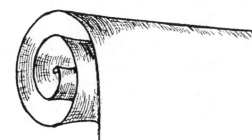

BIBLE DOCTRINE

FOR

YOUNGER CHILDREN

BOOK B

CHAPTERS 11-20

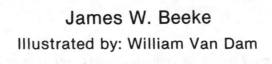

James W. Beeke

Illustrated by: William Van Dam

2008 Reprint Published by
Reformation Heritage Books
2965 Leonard St., NE
Grand Rapids, MI 49525
USA
616-977-0599 / Fax 616-285-3246
e-mail: orders@heritagebooks.org
website: www.heritagebooks.org

ISBN #s: *Bible Doctrine for...*
...Younger Children: Book A   978-1-60178-048-5
...Younger Children: Book B   978-1-60178-049-2
...Older Children: Book A   978-1-60178-050-8
...Older Children: Book B   978-1-60178-051-5

PREFACE

... ACKNOWLEDGMENTS

Dear Friends,

The publication of **Bible Doctrine for Older Children, Books A and B,** is the result of the combined efforts of numerous people. It is not the product of one person.

I wish to sincerely thank everyone who helped in the following ways:

Administrative assistance throughout all phases of production —	Mrs. Jennie Luteyn and Mr. Bob Menger
Art Work —	Mr. William Van Dam
Proof-reading for Scriptural and doctrinal content—	Rev. J. R. Beeke, Rev. A.M. Den Boer, Rev. A. W. Verhoef, Elders J. Beeke, Sr., H. Bisschop, J. De Bruine, L. Den Boer, J. Den Bok, B. Elshout, G. Moerdyk, R. Wierks, and the NRC Book and Publishing Committee
General proof-reading —	Mrs. Jacqueline Markus and the teaching faculty of Timothy Christian School
Typing, type-setting, lay-out, and printing —	Mrs. Arlene Hoefakker, Miss Lisa Neels and Mrs. Bernita Van Hierden
Use and critical review of the first draft edition —	Principals and teachers of the Netherlands Reformed Christian Schools throughout United States and Canada
Constant support and co-operation —	The NRC Synodical Education Committee members, the NRC Book and Publishing Committee, and the Timothy Christian School Board and faculty members
Understanding, patience, and loving assistance—	My wife, Ruth

Above all, may we together acknowledge the Lord, who has graciously provided the opportunity and means to produce these textbooks. May He savingly apply the truths taught therein to the hearts of their readers. May His name receive all the honor and glory — for He is so worthy to be praised!

The need for simple, clear doctrinal teachings is very great. It is my sincere desire that the Lord will bless these books and use them as a means to clearly teach the truths of Scripture to our children. "That we henceforth be no more children, tossed to and fro, and carried about with every wind of doctrine, by the sleight of men, and cunning craftiness, whereby they lie in wait to deceive; but speaking the truth in love, may grow up into Him in all things, which is the Head, even Christ (Ephesians 4:14-15)."

Further, may God bless the study of biblical doctrine internally. Only through the inward working and application of the Holy Spirit will anyone ever be taught these truths in his soul. As Paul writes, "I have planted, Apollos watered; but God gave the increase. So then neither is he that planteth any thing, neither he that watereth; but God that giveth the increase (I Corinthians 3:6-7)."

— J. W. Beeke

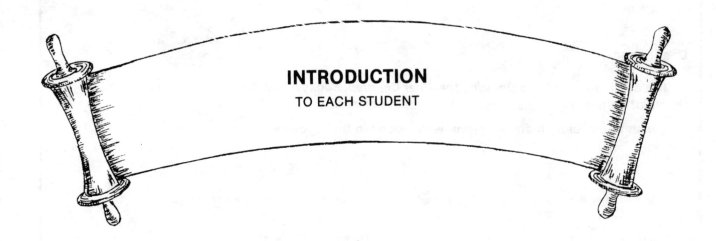

INTRODUCTION
TO EACH STUDENT

Dear Students,

Have you ever received a letter from an important person? If so, you probably read this letter carefully. You were very interested in what this person had written to you.

The Bible is the most important letter in the world. It was written by God and sent to us to read. The Bible is God's Word. It teaches God's truths. These truths are called Bible doctrines.

You will need to read and study the Bible and its doctrines very carefully. The Bible is the most important letter you will ever receive, for it was written by God Himself.

As you begin studying Bible doctrine — do so seriously. Read and study each lesson carefully. Pray and ask God to teach you His truths. Ask God to work in your heart — to bless these truths in your life. God can plant spiritual life within you and turn you from a deep love of sin to a true love of Him.

May God bless you personally as you study His truths in this book.

TABLE OF CONTENTS

Book B
Chapters 11-20

Chapter	Subject	Page Number
11	Calling Regeneration Conversion	6
12	Faith Types of Faith	16
13	Justification Sanctification	30
14	Prayer	42
15	The Church The Church Offices	57
16	Doctrinal Standards Creeds The Five Points of Calvinism	68
17	The Means of Grace God's Word God's Sacraments	84
18	Holy Baptism	96
19	The Lord's Supper	116
20	The Soul After Death Christ's Second Coming The Resurrection of the Dead The Final Judgment Eternity	130

For a complete index of catechism questions and
acknowledgements of source credits used throughout the twenty
chapters in this series, see pages 154-155.

CHAPTER 11

CALLING
REGENERATION
CONVERSION

NEW WORDS

1. Outward call — God's call to all who hear His Word to turn from sin and seek Him

2. Inward call — An all-powerful (or irresistible) call by the Holy Spirit through the Word of God that works salvation in the hearts of those who are saved

3. Regeneration — The planting by God of new spiritual life in the heart of a spiritually dead sinner

4. Conversion — The turning of a person by God from a love of sin to a love of God

5. New heart — A new nature given by God in regeneration which seeks to love God and hates sin

6. Born again — The state of having a new nature and spiritual life from God

7. Experience — Something we have learned from that which has happened to or within us

8. Scheme — Plan

9. Heart — The spiritual part of man; his soul; where his deepest loves, desires, thoughts, and wants are

10. Spiritual — Having to do with the heart or soul of a person and his relationship with God

WHAT DO YOU THINK?

DANGER AHEAD!

Imagine finding a dangerous power line which has fallen across your street. You quickly run up the street to warn any approaching cars.

You soon meet a friend's family approaching in their car. You stop them and warn them to turn around. But they just laugh and drive on up the dangerous street far too fast to stop in time. How would you feel? Why?

Your teacher warns you to turn from the dangerous road of sin. If you just laugh and keep on going far too fast to ever stop in time, how will your teacher feel? Why?

God calls you in many ways to turn from the dangerous way of sin. Have you listened to these warnings?

Seek ye the LORD while He may be found, **call ye upon Him** while He is near: Let the wicked forsake his way, and the unrighteous man his thoughts: and let him return unto the LORD, and He will have mercy upon him; and to our God, for He will abundantly pardon.

— Isaiah 55:6-7

And a certain woman named Lydia, a seller of purple, of the city of Thyatira, which worshipped God heard us: **whose heart the Lord opened,** that she attended unto the things which were spoken of Paul.

— Acts 16:14

CALLING

God created us to love Him and others. Through our sinful fall in Adam, we no longer love or serve God. We now hate God and love ourselves, sin, Satan, and the world.

God calls to warn us that we are going in the wrong direction. We are on a dangerous path. God calls us through the sermons we hear in church. He calls us through the Bible lessons we study in school and catechism class. We are called when we read or hear the Bible at home. We are called through the different happenings in our lives.

We may have an accident, become sick, or have something very wonderful happen to us. God calls to us in all these ways. He calls us to turn from sin to loving and serving Him. This calling of God is named God's **outward call.** God's outward call comes to all who hear His Word. God's outward call should stop us. We should listen, but our **hearts** are so sinful that we will not and do not stop. We stubbornly go on in our own way. We continue in loving and serving sin, Satan, and the world. Isn't this sad?

We need another kind of call from God to stop us on our sinful way. We need a deeper calling of God to save us. The Holy Spirit must bring this call powerfully into our souls. This all-powerful call is named God's **inward call.**

God's inward call stops a person on his sinful way. The Holy Spirit plants new **spiritual** life in him. This planting of new spiritual life is called **regeneration.**

REGENERATION

Man was created to love, honor, and serve God. Through our deep fall in Adam, however, we are now all born spiritually dead. We no longer love or serve God. We go in an opposite direction.

We are now separated from God. Therefore, we do not know, love, serve, or honor God. We do not walk in His way.

We all need regeneration. We need God to plant new spiritual life in us. Another name for this new spiritual birth is "regeneration" or "being **born again**."

> Jesus answered and said unto him, Verily, verily, I say unto thee, Except a man be **born again,** he cannot see the kingdom of God.
>
> — John 3:3

Only the Holy Spirit can place new spiritual life in a person. Only God can plant new spiritual thoughts, desires, and feelings in a person to love and serve Him rather than himself and sin.

Being regenerated or born again is a most wonderful thing! Those who are born again desire to worship and serve God. Their "new hearts" desire to fulfill the purpose for which they were created.

God can freely give this gift. He delights to save lost sinners. Have you asked God for a **new heart?** Do you know anything of this new life? If not, are you seriously praying and asking God for regeneration?

> A **new heart** also will I give you, and a **new spirit** will I put within you: and I will take away the stony heart out of your flesh, and I will give you an heart of flesh. And I will put My Spirit within you, and cause you to walk in My statutes, and ye shall keep My judgments, and do them.
>
> —Ezekiel 36:26-27

WHAT DO YOU THINK?

WE NEED LIGHT

Mr. Moffat was a missionary to Bechuanaland in Africa.

He describes the darkness of a Bechuana village on the nights when there was no moon. "This darkness was something very striking and sad. The climate was too hot for the natives to have a fire in their huts. They just had to 'sit in darkness,' as the Bible says."

Can you imagine how sad this would be? There was darkness everywhere. The frightening roars of wild animals sounded very close. But as the Holy Spirit foretold long ago, "The people that walked in darkness have seen a great light."

The people learned to make candles and prepare oil for lamps. Then they received natural light. The dark evenings in their houses became bright and cheerful like our own.

Some of the Bechuanas were brought by God to believe in the Savior, Jesus Christ. They received spiritual light and a hope for the world to come.

What two types of "light" did these African people receive? Which kind is more important? Why?

— Adapted from *The NRC Banner of Truth*

9

CONVERSION

When God regenerates or gives a new spiritual life, then that person also receives **conversion** from the Lord. If something is converted, it is changed over or turned around. When a person is converted, God turns him from loving sin to loving God. His deepest longings, desires, and feelings are turned away from loving self, sin, the world, and Satan. His deepest desires are now to love God and others. This person now wants to flee from the sin he used to love. He **experiences** a true love for God and his neighbor.

A regenerated person needs to experience conversion for the first time. But, he must also experience conversion continually in his daily life. He needs to be continually turned from serving sin to serving God.

A simple sketch may help to explain this. Follow steps 1, 2, and 3 in the drawing below.

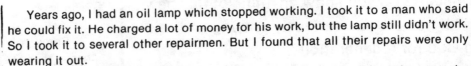

2. God plants new spiritual life in a person (regeneration).

3. The person is now turned and desires to love, serve, and honor God (conversion).

Love:
God
My neighbor

Love:
Self   World
Sin   Satan

1. Before conversion, a person loves self, sin, world, and Satan

To open their eyes, and **to turn them from darkness to light,** and from the power of Satan unto God, that they may receive forgiveness of sins, and inheritance among them which are sanctified by faith that is in Me.

— Acts 26:18

And said, Verily I say unto you, Except ye **be converted,** and become as little children, ye shall not enter into the kingdom of heaven.

—Matthew 18:3

That ye **put off** concerning the former conversation **the old man,** which is corrupt according to the deceitful lusts;

And be renewed in the spirit of your mind;

And that ye **put on the new man,** which after God is created in righteousness and true holiness.

—Ephesians 4:22-24

WHAT DO YOU THINK?

ONLY IT'S MAKER CAN FIX IT

Years ago, I had an oil lamp which stopped working. I took it to a man who said he could fix it. He charged a lot of money for his work, but the lamp still didn't work. So I took it to several other repairmen. But I found that all their repairs were only wearing it out.

At last, I brought it where I should have taken it first. I took it to the man who made it. He soon fixed the lamp and returned it. Now it worked perfectly and burned brightly again.

It is the same with your heart. Your heart needs "fixing" too. You may go to many doctors, you may try to fix it yourself, but it will only get worse.

To whom must your soul be brought? Who made you? Who only can save you? Do you feel your need for Him in your life? Are you seeking the only Savior?

— Adapted from *The NRC Banner of Truth*

WHAT DO YOU THINK?

THE WIDOW'S SON

A God-fearing widow was left with only one son. She had taught him from the Bible and prayed with him since he was a child. But he caused her much sadness for he grew up to be a disobedient boy. He laughed at his mother's warnings and tears. Yet she continued to pray for him.

As he grew older, he went from bad to worse. Finally, he fell into the hands of a judge. As was the custom then, he was whipped, branded with a red-hot iron, and put in prison. Still his mother continued to pray for him to the almighty God.

At last, he was freed from prison. He signed up for service on a ship where no one would know him. He lived a very rough life at sea for some time. One day, a terrible storm smashed the ship against some rocks. The ship was broken into pieces and the whole crew died. Only the praying mother's son was spared. Covered with wounds, he landed on the shore of an island.

Some heathen natives found the ship-wrecked young man. They gave him some food and drink and locked him in a hut. Soon it was time for the people of this island to celebrate a terrible feast to honor their sea-god idol. Each year they chose the best-looking person on the island to kill as an offering to their idol. Now this "whiteman" was the best offering they could ever give. They brought him out and stripped him. As a naked offering, he must die a terrible

death. What went on in this man's heart? Death was before him now!

Suddenly great fear came upon the natives. They could see scars from the whip and the mark of the branding iron on his chest and back. They could not give a blemished offering! They had to set the young man free.

The trembling man hid in a coconut tree which gave him food and drink until he could signal to a passing ship. The sailors took him on board. By God's direction, the ship was sailing to his native land. The captain gave him a place in the bottom of the ship and forgot about him.

Left in this lonely place, the Holy Spirit caused him to begin to think deeply. He remembered the many dangers through which God's goodness had brought him. He remembered his dear mother's warnings, tears, and prayers. This was the time of God's pleasure, the time of his conversion. God now chose to answer the prayers of his God-fearing mother.

He received a broken heart. An old seaman gave him a Bible. He read chapter after chapter as one who is most hungry and thirsty. The Holy Spirit blessed what he read to his heart.

Out of his deep misery he cried continually, "My sins, oh, my sins!" He kneeled again and again and prayed, "Show mercy to me, Oh God! Show mercy to me a great sinner! Oh hear my prayer!" He was driven to the Lord Jesus and His forgiving blood. After a short but fearful struggle, he found peace in Christ. Oh, if only his mother was still living! If only she could know that her prayers were now answered!

When he finally returned home and found his mother, what type of meeting do you think they had?

Can you see God's power in this story? Can you see true conversion? When conversion is true in a person's life, how will his life be different from what it was before?

— Adapted from *Religious Stories for Young and Old*

WHAT DO YOU THINK?

THE POWER OF A SHORT SERMON

A soldier in the British army was very disobedient. He caused several problems. The commander tried to change the soldier's behavior. At last, however, he had to put the soldier in prison. He was put in solitary confinement — a small room where he was totally alone.

This soldier was usually very loud and fun-loving. This forced silence and darkness were torture for him. Two weeks passed by. He passed the long hours in bitter swearing against God.

The army minister tried to speak with this man several times. Every **scheme** he tried would not help. Finally, he gave up. Then another old minister visited him. He tried to pray for this man, but the man kept yelling and swearing so loudly that neither the man nor the minister could hear the prayer.

The old minister could not speak with the man so he prepared to leave. At the door he turned and gave the soldier a hard, searching look. The light from the open door shone on the minister's face in a remarkable way. The startled prisoner stopped yelling to look at him. The minister quickly took this opportunity to sternly say, "Young man, the wages of sin is death."

The door clanged shut. The minister left, but his words did not. The Holy Spirit applied these words with power to his soul. Over and over those words burned in the heart of the soldier — "The wages of sin is death; The wages of sin is death." Finally, after much soul struggle and pain, the soldier dropped to his knees and cried out, "God be merciful to me a sinner."

Later, the soldier learned the last part of the verse which the minister had quoted — "but the gift of God is eternal life, through Jesus Christ our Lord." What a wonder this was for him! Salvation was possible, even for such a great sinner as he!

The soldier's conversion was real and lasting. He lived to be a good soldier of Jesus Christ. He loved to speak of the grace of God for unworthy sinners.

Can you see true conversion taking place in the life of this soldier? What did this man love before his conversion? Whom does he love most deeply after his conversion? Will he love and desire to serve sin or God in his future life? Why?

— Adapted from *Religious Stories for Young and Old*

A person who is converted is not perfectly sinless in this life upon earth. A regenerated person has two natures in his heart; the old sinful nature with which he was born, and a new nature which was given by God in regeneration. These two natures fight to pull the person in opposite directions. The following sketch will help picture this truth:

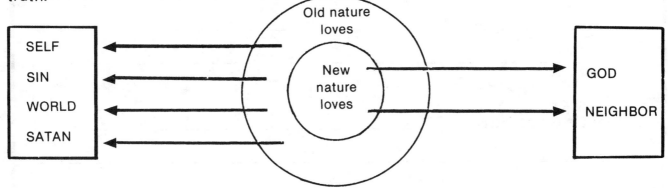

Heart of a regenerated person

There is a spiritual war taking place inside the heart of a converted person. When he dies his old nature will stay in the grave, but the new nature will rejoice in victory with God forever in heaven.

Do you know something of new spiritual life from God? Do you love to serve God? Do you fight against sin? If so, may God strengthen you to serve Him more and more in all things. If not, your condition is most dangerous. You canot be saved without being born again of God. Salvation is all from God. Therefore earnestly pray and plead with God for regeneration and conversion. God can and will save lost sinners. He is a wonderfully gracious God!

MEMORIZATION QUESTIONS

1. What is it to be truly converted?
   It is receiving a new heart. Ezekiel 36:26

2. Who can give us this?
   God only. Luke 18:27

3. What is it to receive a new heart?
   To love God above all.

4. Wherein does this further consist?
   In a hatred of sin, which naturally accompanies it. Psalm 139:21

5. Wherein must we hate sin?
   In its first cause. Romans 7:7

6. What is it to serve God?
   To surrender soul and body to Him with submission to His will. I Corinthians 6:20

7. How can this come to pass?
   By being born again. John 3:4, 5

8. What is it to be born again?
   It is a complete change of man in all his inclinations. Ephesians 4:22, 23, 24

9. Who can do this?
   God, by His Word and Spirit. Titus 3:5

10. How must we love the Lord?
    With all our heart. Proverbs 23:26

11. To whom have we given our hearts?
    To Satan and the world.

Ledeboer's Catechism: Q. 27-31, 38-41, 58-59

CHAPTER CHECK-UP

1. What is God's *outward call?* _____

_____

_____

2. What is God's *inward call?* _____

_____

_____

3. What is regeneration? _____

_____

_____

4. Why do we all need to be spiritually born again?

_____

_____

_____

5. What is conversion? _____

_____

_____

6. Before conversion, what do we love and serve in our lives?

a. _____

b. _____

c. _____

d. _____

CHAPTER CHECK-UP

7. What are a person's deepest desires after conversion?

    a. _____

    b. _____

8. a. After regeneration, can a person love God perfectly in his life on earth?____

    b. Why or why not? _____

    _____

9. In the heart of a regenerated person, whom or what does:

    a. The new nature love most deeply? _____

    _____

    b. The old nature love most deeply? _____

    _____

10. Why is there a "spiritual war" in the heart of a regenerated person? _____

    _____

    _____

11. a. When will all converted people gain the victory over their old natures? ____

    _____

    b. Why? _____

    _____

12. How does God in conversion turn a person's heart back to the same direction

    man was facing before he fell in Paradise?

    _____

    _____

    _____

CHAPTER 12

FAITH
TYPES OF FAITH

NEW WORDS

1. Faith — A belief and trust in someone or something

2. Historical faith — A belief in the truths of the Bible with the mind only

3. Temporary faith — A belief in God with mind and feelings for a short time

4. Miraculous faith — A belief that a miracle will be done by or for us

5. True saving faith — A belief and trust in God and His way of salvation with the whole heart through the work of the Holy Spirit

6. Salvation — God's deliverance of His people through Jesus Christ from spiritual and eternal death and His gift of spiritual and eternal life

7. Misery — The extremely sad and poor condition sinners are in because of their sin

8. Deliverance — Salvation through Jesus Christ; being saved from the greatest misery and brought into the greatest good

9. Thankfulness — Gratitude; full of desire to serve, honor, and walk in God's way out of love to God for His merciful deliverance

10. Mercy — Love to someone in a miserable condition who does not deserve it

FAITH

What is *faith?* Faith is belief and trust in someone or something. If we believe that someone is telling us the truth, we have faith in that person. But faith is more than just believing. It is also trusting. Read the "What Do You Think?" on this page. You can stand on solid ground and say, "I believe that the bridge will hold me." How is that different from believing that it will hold you when you actually walk over it?

WHAT DO YOU THINK?

THE SHAKY BRIDGE

Look at this shaky bridge. It is tied to some trees high over a rushing river. If a person said, "I have faith that this bridge will hold me and bring me safely to the other side," what do you think would be the best way to test his faith?

KING AGRIPPA

In Acts 26, we read that Paul spoke to King Agrippa, and said in verse 27:

> King Agrippa, believest thou the prophets? I know that thou believest.

How did King Agrippa answer? We read in verse 28:

> Then Agrippa said unto Paul, Almost thou persuadest me to be a Christian.

King Agrippa believed in his mind the history of Jesus' life. But he did not have a heartfelt need to be delivered from his sin through the saving work of Jesus Christ. What type of faith did King Agrippa have?

The Bible speaks of four kinds or types of faith. These four kinds are:

1. Historical faith
2. Temporary faith
3. Miraculous faith
4. True saving faith

What is **historical faith?** The word "historical" comes from the word "history." Historical faith means to believe the history of the Bible. People with historical faith believe that what is written in the Bible is true. But there is no interest in or need for the teachings of the Bible. They believe that the Bible is true, but these truths do not become their main concern.

Think back to the bridge over the rushing river. Picture one side of the river as sin and death, and the other side as spiritual life with God. The bridge from sin to God is the Lord Jesus Christ. People with only historical faith believe in their **minds** that there is such a bridge, but they are not wholeheartedly inter - rested in it. They do not feel in their hearts a great need to be delivered from their sin. Therefore, they do not value this bridge. They do not feel their need to be delivered by Jesus Christ.

Probably each of you has historical faith. This is a great blessing. You need to know the Word of God and believe that it is true in your mind. You need to learn more of the truths and history of the Bible all the time. But to be saved, you need more than historical faith. You must learn to know your sin in such a way that it becomes real. It must become a heart-felt burden. There must be a true need for deliverance. God shows you that most wonderful bridge, the Lord Jesus Christ. You will feel a great need and see such a value in that "Bridge." You will give up everything to be brought across that "Bridge" and find friendship with God. Experiencing this by actually crossing the "Bridge" is different from just knowing about it. To be saved, you need more than just historical faith.

What is *temporary faith?* The word "temporary" means "only for some time." It is something which does not last. Temporary faith lasts only for awhile. Temporary faith is deeper than historical faith. Not only the mind of the person, but also his feelings are active in temporary faith. For awhile it seems like this is true saving faith. But later, especially when the person must give up things or suffer difficulties, temporary faith disappears. Temporary faith includes the *mind and the feelings* of a person, but not his heart. The deepest loves, desires, and feelings are not changed. His heart is not turned from a deep love of self and sin to God. Such a person does not truly need the "Bridge," Jesus Christ. He is not actually brought across it. For awhile it looks like he might cross, but when tested, he goes back.

What is *miraculous faith?* The word "miraculous" comes from the word "miracle." It means "having faith in miracles." Miraculous faith is a strong belief that a miracle will be done by or for a person.

There were many people who came to the Lord Jesus and to His apostles with only a faith in miracles. They believed that Jesus or His apostles could heal them. But they did not feel their great need to be healed from their spiritual sickness of sin. They, too, had a type of faith — a faith in miracles. But they did not value the "Bridge" which leads from sin to God. They had no felt need for their deliverance from sin.

WHAT DO YOU THINK?

RUTH AND ORPAH

You know the story of Ruth, Orpah, and Naomi, don't you? When Naomi returned to the land of Israel, both girls wanted to go with her. They both said, "Surely we will return with thee unto thy people." It seemed as though both girls really meant it. They both said this with tears.

The final test came at the border. When Orpah heard what she would have to give up and leave behind if she went over the border with Naomi, she went back to Moab. Orpah returned to her former people and gods.

Ruth, however, did not go back. Even though she had to give up the same things as Orpah, Ruth said to Naomi:

> Intreat me not to leave thee, or to return from following after thee: for whither thou goest, I will go; and where thou lodgest, I will lodge: thy people shall be my people, and *thy God my God:*
> Where thou diest, I will die, and there will I be buried: the LORD do so to me, and more also, if ought but death part thee and me.
> —Ruth 1:16-17

What type of faith do you think Orpah had? What type of faith did Ruth have?

THE TEN LEPERS

Once Jesus entered a certain village where ten lepers met Him. We read that "they lifted up their voices, and said, 'Jesus, Master, have mercy on us.' "

Jesus sent them to see the priests, and on their way they were healed. Then we read:

And one of them, when he saw that he was healed, turned back, and with a loud voice glorified God,

And fell down on his face at His feet, giving Him thanks: and he was a Samaritan.

And Jesus answering said, Were there not ten cleansed? but where are the nine?

There are not found that returned to give glory to God, save this stranger.

— Luke 17:15-18

Only one leper needed Jesus to heal his soul. He was healed from his bodily disease but he came back and fell at Jesus' feet. All ten lepers believed Jesus could heal their bodies. What type of faith did the other nine lepers have?

They only wanted to be healed from bodily sickness. Their hearts were not changed. They were not brought across the "Bridge," Jesus Christ, from death to life.

What is **true saving faith?** True saving faith is a belief and trust with the whole heart in God's **salvation** through Jesus Christ. True saving faith is a gift of God worked in a person's heart by the Holy Spirit. His **heart is converted.** He is renewed and turned from loving self and sin to loving God. He receives a new heart from God.

A person who receives true saving faith has a heartfelt need to find the Lord Jesus Christ. He must find that "Bridge" from sin to God. He cannot rest until he has been brought into favor with God through Jesus Christ.

WHAT DO YOU THINK?

And though I have all faith, so that I could remove mountains, and have not charity, I am nothing.

— I Corinthians 13:2b

What type of faith is Paul speaking of here?

True saving faith shows itself through the good works done by people who have received this faith. They now love to serve God. He is their new Master and King. They love to do His will more than their own. God's will is taught in His Word — the Bible. Those who receive true saving faith desire to walk in the way of God. They follow God's Word and law,

not only because they have to, but because they want to. Their hearts love to serve and obey God, their new King.

True saving faith is not only in the **mind** and **feelings** of a person. It is deeply felt in his **heart.** His deepest thoughts, desires, and loves are converted. How does a person experience this?

True saving faith is experienced in the way of:

1. Misery
2. Deliverance
3. Thankfulness

Misery means that a person experiences that he is without God in the world. He is a lost sinner who cannot save himself. This experience is worked in his heart by the Holy Spirit. This causes him to cry out for **deliverance.** God then shows him that Jesus Christ is the only way of escape from his misery. Jesus Christ is the only Deliverer for such a helplessly lost sinner. He then hopes, trusts, and clings

WHAT DO YOU THINK?

THE GROUND UPON WHICH THE SEED FELL

The Lord Jesus once told a story about a man who planted seeds in his field. These seeds fell on different kinds of ground. This was a picture of the Word of God falling on different types of hearts. You can read this story in:

Matthew 13:3-9

And He spake many things unto them in parables, saying, Behold a sower went forth to sow:

And when he sowed, some seeds fell by the way side, and the fowls came and devoured them up:

Some fell upon stony places, where they had not much earth: and forthwith they sprung up, because they had not deepness of earth:

And when the sun was up, they were scorched; and because they had no root, they withered away.

And some fell among thorns; and the thorns sprung up, and choked them:

But other fell into good ground, and brought forth fruit, some an hundredfold, some sixtyfold, some thirtyfold.

Who hath ears to hear, let him hear.

Which ground do you think is a picture of true saving faith? How do you know?

WHAT DO YOU THINK?

ARE YOU SAVED?

Have you ever been swimming at a lake where there was a life-guard? If so, you probably did not value this life-guard very highly. Maybe you hardly even noticed him. Why didn't you value the life-guard? Because you did not feel that you needed him. You were having fun and thought that everything was going well.

But what would happen if you swam out into deep water and suddenly had a leg cramp — a cramp so tight that you could not move? You tried everything you could to stay above water, but you started to sink. You cried out, "Help! Help! Help me!" You felt yourself starting to sink. You went under, but came up again. For the second time your head came above water. In despair, you cried out again. Through blurred eyes, you saw the life-guard coming closer. He grabbed you and held you firmly. Suddenly there was hope! You clung to him. You trusted that he could save you from sinking.

This was the same life-guard that you did not see any value in before. Why did you value him later? Did the life-guard change? No, but you experienced a felt need for this life-guard. You experienced that you would die without him.

This story can be used as an example of how we experience spiritual misery and deliverance in our hearts. The Savior, Jesus Christ, is preached to us every Sunday. But by nature we feel no need for this Savior and see little value in Him. But if we experience misery, if it becomes true that we are sinking and will die in sin, then that Savior becomes most valuable! Then we will cry out for Him! We will cling to Him as the only and most wonderful way of deliverance.

Do you think such a person would be thankful to God for saving him? How would he show his thankfulness in his life? Have you experienced spiritual misery, deliverance, and thankfulness?

to this Savior. His heart overflows with **thankfulness** to God for this wonderful deliverance. His thankfulness to God is shown by walking in God's way.

God receives all the honor for saving a lost sinner. Each converted person knows that, in himself, he is only a sinner and deserves to die. It was, and is, only God's **mercy** that saves him. Have you received true saving faith from God? Have you experienced something of misery, deliverance, and thankfulness in your life? Has your heart been renewed by God to love Him above all? If so, do you continually need the Lord to turn you more and more from sin to Him? If not, are you continually praying and seeking God for this? To be saved, we need to receive true saving faith from God.

WHAT DO YOU THINK?

"MINE'S A RELIGION FOR ALL WEATHERS"

There was a village on the Cornish Coast where the people were very poor. They were intelligent, God-fearing people. In 1859, they were troubled by such strong winds that the men could not go out fishing for nearly a month. At last on a Sunday morning, the wind changed. Some of the men went down to launch to their fishing boats. Their wives and children looked on sadly. Many shook their heads and said, "It's too bad that it's Sunday, but . . . if only we were not so poor. . ."

"But — if!" said a strong fisherman who joined the group on the shore. "Surely, neighbors, you are not going with your 'buts' and 'ifs' to break God's law!"

The people gathered around him and he added, "Mine's a religion for all weathers, fair wind and foul. 'This is the love of God, that we keep His commandments.' 'Remember the Sabbath Day to keep it holy.' That's the law, friends; our Lord came not to break, but to fulfill the law. True, we are poor; but what of that? Better poor and have God's smile, than rich and have His frown. Go, you that dare, but I never knew any good that came of a religion that changed with the wind."

These wise words had

These wise words had their effect. All went home and dressed for church instead. The day was spent in worshipping God. In the evening, just when the boats would have been returning had they gone out, a sudden storm arose. It raged terribly for two whole days. After that came several days of calm weather. During this time, they caught so much fish that there was no more complaining in the village. Here was a religion for all weathers.

Is your religion a "religion for all weathers"? True saving faith desires to serve God at all times.

— Adapted from *The NRC Banner of Truth*

MEMORIZATION QUESTIONS

1. What is the greatest misery?
   Not to feel our misery. Revelation 3:17

2. Is that necessary?
   Yes, Jeremiah 3:13, "Only acknowledge thine iniquity."

3. How do we come to that knowledge?
   By the discovering light of the Holy Spirit.

4. Wherein does this true knowledge reveal itself?
   In the knowledge of one's own guilt and in the approval of God's punishment. Psalm 51:3,4

5. What is believing?
   Trusting in God with all the heart through the Holy Ghost. Hebrews 11:1

6. Is it enough to say, I believe?
   No, we must repent. Matthew 7:21

7. What is repentance?
   To better one's life. Matthew 3:8

8. Wherein does repentance consist?
   Ceasing to do evil and doing what is good by faith. Isaiah 1:16,17

Questions 1-4: Ledeboer's Catechism Q. 15-18

5-8: Borstius' Catechism Lesson XXIII, Q. 3-6

CHAPTER CHECK-UP

1. What is faith? _____
    _____
    _____

2. Name the four kinds of faith and a person or people in the Bible who are examples of these types:

    Kind of Faith   **Biblical Example**

    a. _____   _____
    b. _____   _____
    c. _____   _____
    d. _____   _____

3. How is historical faith different from temporary faith? _____
    _____
    _____

4. How is true saving faith different from all other kinds of faith? _____
    _____
    _____
    _____

5. If a person has received true saving faith from God, how can this be seen in his life? _____
    _____

6. Who works true saving faith in the hearts of sinners? _____
    _____

CHAPTER CHECK-UP

7. The experience of true religion and true saving faith includes the following three parts:

    a. _____

    b. _____

    c. _____

8. Why is it necessary to experience our sinful misery? _____

    _____

    _____

    _____

9. Why is the Savior, Jesus Christ, so valuable to those who have learned that they are totally lost sinners? _____

    _____

    _____

10. Would a converted person follow God's law only because he "had to" or also because he "wanted to"? _____

    Why? _____

    _____

    _____

11. Who deserves all the honor when a sinner is saved? Why? _____

    _____

    _____

CHAPTER ELEVEN

REVIEW QUESTIONS

1. How is God's inward call different from His outward call? _____

   _____

   _____

   _____

2. What is regeneration? _____

   _____

   _____

3. Who works regeneration? _____

4. a. What is a person's deepest love and desire before conversion?

      _____

   b. What is a person's deepest love and desire after conversion?

      _____

5. Why are there two natures in the heart of a regenerated person? _____

   _____

   _____

6. Name the two natures of a regenerated person on this drawing. Draw arrows to show which way each nature is pulling this person.

The heart of a regenerated person

Love:
God
Neighbor

Love:
Self
Sin
Satan
World

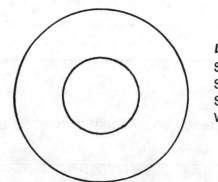

7. Name two parts of faith:

    a. _____

    b. _____

8. Match the following by drawing a line to the correct answer:

    a. Historical faith   A belief in God for a time, but without a true
                                    change of heart

    b. Temporary faith   A wholehearted belief and trust in God

    c. Miraculous faith   A belief in the truths of the Bible with the mind
                                    only

    d. True saving faith   A belief that a miracle will be done by or for us

9. What will be seen in the lives of those who have been given true saving faith?

    _____

    _____

    _____

10. What three things are experienced in true saving faith?

    a. _____

    b. _____

    c. _____

11. a. Why is it necessary to experience misery before deliverance? _____

    _____

    b. Why is it necessary to experience deliverance before thankfulness? _____

    _____

    _____

CROSSWORD PUZZLE

Use the twenty NEW WORDS found in Chapters 11 and 12 to complete this crossword puzzle.

Across

2. The spiritual part of man; his soul
4. God's call to turn from sin to Him
7. Plan
8. Something we have learned from that which has happened to us
9. A belief and trust in God with the whole heart through the work of the Holy Spirit
11. Having to do with the heart of a person and his relationship with God
13. God's planting new spiritual life in the heart of a spiritually dead sinner
16. A belief in the truths of the Bible with the mind only
17. A new nature, given by God in regeneration, which seeks to love and serve God
19. A belief in God with mind and feelings for a short time

Down

1. Gratitude
3. The state of having a new nature from God; a new spiritual life
5. A belief that a miracle will be done by or for me
6. Love to someone who does not deserve it
7. God's deliverance of His people from eternal death and His gift to them of eternal life
10. An all-powerful calling in the heart of those who are saved by the Holy Spirit through His Word
12. The turning of a person by God from serving self and sin to God
14. Belief and trust
15. Salvation through Jesus Christ; being saved from the greatest misery and brought into the greatest good.
18. The poor and sad condition sinners are in due to their fall and totally sinful hearts

BIBLE STUDY QUESTIONS

Draw a line to connect each doctrinal truth with the text which most clearly teaches this truth.

Doctrinal Truths

1. God calls us to turn from sin unto Him.

2. Of ourselves we will not seek or turn to God.

3. We need to be spiritually born again by God.

4. We need to be converted from a deep love of sin to God.

5. True saving faith knows and confesses its sin before God.

6. Miraculous faith believes in a miracle of God but does not have true love to God.

7. True saving faith brings forth fruits of good works.

Texts

A. **John 3:3**
Jesus answered and said unto him, Verily, verily, I say unto thee, Except a man be born again, he cannot see the kingdom of God.

B. **Ephesians 4:22-24**
That ye put off concerning the former conversation the old man, which is corrupt according to the deceitful lusts;
And be renewed in the spirit of your mind;
And that ye put on the new man, which after God is created in righteousness and true holiness.

C. **I Corinthians 13:2b**
And though I have all faith, so that I could remove mountains, and have not charity, I am nothing.

D. **Isaiah 55:6-7**
Seek ye the LORD while He may be found, call ye upon Him while He is near:
Let the wicked forsake his way, and the unrighteous man his thoughts: and let him return unto the LORD, and He will have mercy upon him; and to our God, for He will abundantly pardon.

E. **Matthew 13:8**
But other fell into good ground, and brought forth fruit, some an hundredfold, some sixtyfold, some thirtyfold.

F. **Psalm 14:2-3**
The LORD looked down from heaven upon the children of men, to see if there were any that did understand, and seek God.
They are all gone aside, they are all together become filthy: there is none that doeth good, no, not one.

G. **Psalm 51:3-4**
For I acknowledge my transgressions: and my sin is ever before me.
Against Thee, Thee only, have I sinned, and done this evil in Thy sight: that Thou mightest be justified when Thou speakest, and be clear when Thou judgest.

CHAPTER 13

JUSTIFICATION
SANCTIFICATION

NEW WORDS

1. Accusing — Blaming someone for wrong-doing or for sin
2. Defending — Protecting another from his accusers
3. Sentence — A judge's pronouncement of a guilty person's punishment
4. Justification — The forgiveness of the guilt of sin and receipt of a right to eternal life for Christ's sake
5. Debt — That which is owed and must be paid
6. Guilt — The fact of having done wrong or having broken a law
7. Substitute — One who takes the place of another
8. Justice — Fairness; a just reward or punishment given according to what is deserved
9. Benefit — To help or do good to another
10. Sanctification — Being washed by God from the pollution of sin; living in the way of God's commandments after conversion

JUSTIFICATION

WHAT DO YOU THINK?

SPOKEN FREE!

Imagine that you were in a courtroom where you saw a judge, a person being tried, **accusing** witnesses, and a **defending** lawyer. A young man had been brought to court because he drove his car carelessly and hit a parked car. The judge heard all the facts from the accusing witnesses. The young man had nothing to say. He was clearly guilty. What happened was his own fault. He would have to pay the full damages of $2,500. This poor young man did not have any money with which to pay. Yet he was guilty and had to pay the full price. The judge was ready to **sentence** him. What would happen?

Just at that moment the young man's defending lawyer stepped forward. "Sir," he said to the judge, "I will be his mediator. I will pay the full price for this young man!" He then handed over a check for $2,500 to the judge.

The judge accepted this check, turned to the young man, and spoke clearly, "The account is fully paid. I declare you free!"

This man was justified. He was spoken free. Do you think he was happy? What spiritual truth is pictured by this story? This chapter will speak about the forgiveness and payment of a greater debt — an elect sinner's **justification.**

WHAT DO YOU THINK?

JUSTIFIED BY GOD

Many years ago, a man who lived in the town of Ayr, committed several horribly wicked crimes. After he was caught and tried, he was sentenced to death by hanging.

While in prison, God worked wonderfully in the heart of this hardened criminal. He came to see his great sinfulness and misery. He experienced a sore struggle in his heart. Soon after, he came to know his deliverance through the death of Jesus Christ.

The day arrived when he had to be put to death. He could not help but cry out to the gathered crowd, "God is a great forgiver! God is a great forgiver!"

This man's heart overflowed with deep wonder and thankfulness for God's free mercy!

Do you think he knew what justification meant? Did he know this truth only in his mind, or did he also know something of it personally in the experience of his heart?

— Adapted from *The Shorter Catechism Illustrated*

All people are guilty in the sight of God. We are guilty because of our sinful fall in Adam. We are guilty because of our daily sins in thoughts, words, and actions. We all have a **debt** much larger than the debt of the young man in the story you just read. We have a debt so great that we can never pay it back. We have sinned against an infinite God.

Just as the poor man in the story, we have not a penny with which to pay. We only add to our guilt by sinning more each day. God the Father will judge us. What will our sentence be? The wages of sin is death: bodily death, spiritual death, and eternal death.

> For the wages of sin is **death.**
> — Romans 6:23a

> **Cursed** is every one that continueth not in all things which are written in the book of the law to do them.
> — Galatians 3:10b

> Then shall He say also unto them on the left hand, Depart from Me, ye cursed, **into everlasting fire,** prepared for the devil and his angels.
> — Matthew 25:41

Is there no hope? Is there no way of escape? From our side, there is none. But what a great wonder; there is a Lawyer and Mediator who will plead for His people! The Lord Jesus Christ fully paid for the **guilt** of His people. He suffered and died to pay the full price for the sins of His elect children. What a wonderful **Substitute!**

God the Father accepts the full payment of Jesus Christ for sin. Upon this payment, He speaks His children free. God does not pass by His *justice.* His justice is fully satisfied by Christ. This full payment for sin is freely given to His children. This can be pictured as follows:

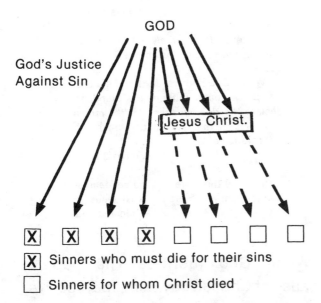

How blessed are those sinners for whom Jesus died! He bore the full wrath of God against sin for them. Christ paid the full price for their sins. God cannot justly punish sin twice. Therefore, God's children are spoken free.

WHAT DO YOU THINK?

THE LITTLE SUBSTITUTE

A teacher once had to punish Tommy for breaking a school rule. For punishment, the guilty boy would have to stand for fifteen minutes in a corner of the room.

As Tommy was going to the corner, a younger boy named Joseph went up to the teacher and asked, "May I take his place?" The teacher agreed. Joseph went, and bore the punishment due to the other boy.

When the time was passed, the teacher called Joseph to him, and asked, "Did Tommy beg you to take his place?"

"No, Sir," he answered.

"Well, don't you think that he deserved to be punished?"

"Yes, Sir; he had broken one of the school rules and he deserved to be punished."

"Why did you want to be punished in his place?"

"Sir, it was because he is my friend and I love him."

The teacher thought this a good opportunity for teaching his students an important lesson.

"Boys and girls," he said, "would it be right for me now to also punish Tommy for breaking the school rules?"

"No, Sir," the class answered.

"Why not?"

"Because his friend, Joseph, was punished in his place."

"Does this remind you of anything?" asked the teacher.

"Yes, Sir," said several voices. "It reminds us that the Lord Jesus bore the punishment for the sins of His people."

"What name would you give to Joseph for what he had done?"

"He was a substitute."

"What is a substitute?"

"One who takes the place of another."

"What place has Jesus taken?"

"That of sinners."

"Joseph has told us that he wished to take his friend's place and be punished instead of him because he loved him. Can you tell me why Jesus wished to die in the place of sinful people?"

"It was because He loves His people who are sinners."

"What passage in the Bible proves this?"

"The Son of God, who loved me, and gave Himself for me," (Galatians 2:20).

Jesus is the most loving of all friends. His people may well say with the hymnwriter,

"One there is, above all others,
Well deserves the name of Friend;
His is love beyond a brother's,
Lasting, true, and knows no end."

Why is Jesus the most wonderful Substitute? What punishment did He have to bear in order to free His people?

— Adapted from *The NRC Banner of Truth*

33

WHAT DO YOU THINK?

FROM A SON OF DEATH TO A SON OF A KING!

You know the story of baby Moses, don't you? All of the Israelite baby boys were sentenced to death.

Why did not Moses die? Why did Moses receive the right to grow up in the king's palace?

You would probably answer by saying that King Pharaoh's daughter adopted Moses. He then became the king's son. In this way, Moses was free from the death of the Israelite boys. He received the right to live in Pharaoh's palace.

God's chosen people are also lost and helpless. But Jesus Christ graciously adopts them as His own children. In this way, they have a right to enter heaven, the palace of God, as His children.

Why are God's children adopted by Jesus Christ? Were they better than other people? Who deserves the honor and glory for their adoption?

To wit, that God was in Christ, reconciling the world unto Himself, *not imputing their trespasses unto them;* and hath committed unto us the word of reconciliation.

For He hath made Him to be sin for us, who knew no sin; that *we might be made the righteousness of God* in Him.

— II Corinthians 5:19,21

Being *justified freely by His grace* through the redemption that is in Christ Jesus:

Whom God hath set forth to be a propitiation through faith in His blood, to declare *His righteousness for the remission of sins* that are past, through the forbearance of God.

— Romans 3:24-25

There is therefore now *no condemnation* to them which are in Christ Jesus.

— Romans 8:1a

When God justifies His people because of Christ's payment, they receive two things:

1. Forgiveness of all sin

2. A right to eternal life as children of God

A sinner's justification can only be based on Jesus Christ and Him crucified. Christ's death, however, does not *benefit* a person unless he is connected to the Savior. A person can only be attached to Jesus Christ by true saving faith.

Do you see your great need for true saving faith? It is neccessary for your life here and for your life to come. Do you continually ask the Lord to work this faith in your heart? Do you daily use the means of grace given by God, the means which He will bless and use for this purpose?

WHAT DO YOU THINK?

THE BLOOD OF THE LAMB

What does this picture show? What happened in Egypt on the Passover night? Why were the Israelites protected? To whom did the killed lamb point? What lesson can we learn from the fact that those who stood behind the lamb's blood were saved? How is this a picture of the justification of God's people through the death of Christ?

Therefore being *justified by faith,* we have peace with God through our Lord Jesus Christ.

— Galatians 2:16

Knowing that a man is not *justified* by the works of the law, but *by the faith of Jesus Christ,* even we have believed in Jesus Christ, that we might be justified by the faith of Christ, and not by the works of the law: for by the works of the law shall no flesh be justified.

— Galatians 2:16

A person who is justified by God is free from the guilt of his sin. But the person is still polluted with the filth of his sin. He also continually needs to be washed from the dirtiness of his daily sin. This washing is called *sanctification.*

SANCTIFICATION

The word "sanctify" means "to become more clean, separated from sin, and devoted to God". Sanctification is being washed by God from the pollution of sin. It means to become more holy. It means to live more according to God's commandments. God the Holy Spirit works in the hearts of His people. God's work of sanctification includes two parts:

1. The death of the old nature

2. The enlivening of the new nature

What do we mean by "the old nature"? What do we mean by "the new nature"? You still remember, don't you?

Sanctification grows out of conversion. If a person's heart is turned toward God in conversion, then his deepest desire is to flee from sin and do that which is pleasing to God. Conversion and sanctification can be pictured by turning a globe. When we turn a globe, it turns *away* from something and turns *toward* something else at the same time. Conversion is the turning; sanctification is the result of the turning — living a life according to God's commandments.

CONVERSION

The heart is turned by God from its deepest love of sin toward God.

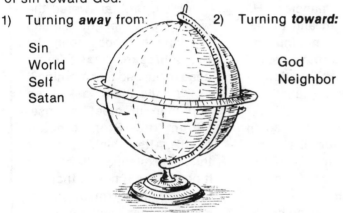

1) Turning *away* from:

Sin
World
Self
Satan

2) Turning *toward:*

God
Neighbor

SANCTIFICATION

Living a holier life; fleeing from sin and doing good works; walking according to God's commandments.

Sanctification is never complete in this life. It is a work of God which begins in the moment of regeneration. It never leaves a child of God during his entire life.

Sanctification has its ups and downs. When the new nature is stronger by God's grace, the fruits of sanctification can be seen. But when the old nature wins out, a child of God falls into sin. This spiritual warfare is taking place in the hearts of all true believers continually. Look back to Chapter 11 and study the picture of this again.

WHAT DO YOU THINK?

DO BABIES GROW?

If we asked, "What do you see in this picture?" you would answer, "A baby."

If we asked, "What is a baby?" you would answer, "A human being, of course."

"If a baby is a human being, it does not have to grow anymore does it?"

"Yes," you answer, "it is a human being, but it still needs to grow in size, strength, and knowledge to become an adult."

This is also true of God's children. They are born as babes in grace. They are true children of God, but they need to grow in sanctification.

As newborn babes desire the sincere milk of the Word: that ye may grow thereby.

— I Peter 2:2

On what "spiritual food" do God's children feed and grow? Who must bless this "food" for their spiritual health?

Sanctify them through Thy truth: Thy word is truth.

And for their sakes I *sanctify* Myself, that they also might be sanctified through the truth.

— John 17:17,19

For this is the will of God, even your *sanctification,* that ye should abstain from fornication.

— I Thessalonians 4:3

And the very God of peace *sanctify* you wholly; and I pray God your whole spirit and soul and body be preserved blameless unto the coming of our Lord Jesus Christ.

— I Thessalonians 5:23

WHAT DO YOU THINK?

POOR JOHN THE STONE-BREAKER

A wealthy Englishman was riding over his estate. Suddenly he stopped his horse. He listened for a moment because he thought he heard someone speaking. Looking over the hedge, he saw a poor man. For many years this poor man had been hired to break stones for the rich man's roads. Therefore, this man was called "John the Stone-breaker."

The rich man called to his poor workman, "I say John, what are you talking to yourself about?"

"Please, Sir," said John, "I wasn't speaking to myself. I was just asking God's blessing on my dinner."

"Ha, ha, ha!" laughed the rich man; "and what have you got for your dinner, John?"

"Well, Sir," replied John, "I've only a crust of bread and a mug of pure water from the brook; but, Sir," he continued, "it's a good meal when God blesses it."

"Well, well," answered his master as he prepared to ride off, "it would be a long time before I'd ask God's blessing on a dinner like that. I wish you much good from the blessing, John. Good day." Away he rode on his tour of inspection.

Still, John enjoyed his dinner in spite of what his wealthy employer had said. The rich man did not know of the wealth which humble John had hidden in his heart. As a true child of God, he had a lasting treasure laid up in heaven.

Not long after this happened, the rich man was taking a short walk in a green field near his mansion. He suddenly jumped and turned pale. He stood trembling with fear — "What's that I hear?" he exclaimed. "The richest man in the county shall die tonight!"

He listened and again thought he heard the same words repeated — "The richest man in the county shall die tonight!"

Greatly alarmed, he began to think of who was the richest man in the county, and finally came to the conclusion that he was.

Hurrying home, he asked for his doctor to come immediately. He seriously asked the doctor to do all he could to save his life. The doctor was very surprised. He did not see anything wrong with his patient. The rich man, however, kept thinking that he was going to die that night.

But why all this excitement? It was the power of the rich man's accusing conscience showing him how unprepared he was to die.

Restlessly, he tossed upon his bed all night. There was no sleep for him. At last the grey dawn appeared. The doctor, who had not left the rich man's side, finally persuaded him to get up and take a walk before breakfast. When he did go out, he was pale and trembling. He expected that at any step he might drop dead.

He had not gone far, however, when he was met by a poor workman who touched his cap respectfully and said, "Please, Sir, may I speak with you?"

"Of course you may," was the reply.

"Well, Sir," answered the workman. "I thought I should tell you that poor John the Stone-breaker was found dead in his bed this morning."

"What's that?" asked the rich man in great surprise, "John the Stone-breaker died!" After thinking about this, he exclaimed, "Ah! I see it now! I see it now! I thought that I, with my many acres, my mansions, and my gold, was the richest man in the county; but poor John the Stone-breaker, with his crust of bread and mug of water, and God's blessing, was by far the richer man."

Whether or not he took this serious lesson to heart, we do not know. God grant, however, that you and I may do so!

Why is justification more valuable than all earthly treasures? How can you see fruits of sanctification in John the Stone-breaker's life? Why was "Poor John" actually very rich? Is it better to be rich in soul or body? Why? Which is of deeper concern to you, your soul or your body?

— Adapted from *The NRC Banner of Truth*

38

God the Holy Spirit dwells in the hearts of His children. He begins and continues their sanctification. Yet the Holy Spirit works sanctification through means. Sometimes God's children slow their growth in sanctification. They should not go to sinful places, keep sinful company, or live selfishly. They should not desire the sinful pleasures of the world, give in to temptations, or yield to other sins. These things are forbidden by God. True believers should actively use God's means of grace. They should carefully study their Bible, listen closely to sermons, and seriously pray for God's blessing. The Holy Spirit will bless the use of these means that His people may grow in sanctification.

Justification and sanctification are always joined together. Those whom God justifies, He also sanctifies. Their sanctification will be seen in good works.

When the love of God is in exercise, His children love to serve God and do that which is pleasing in His sight. They love to obey God and walk according to His law.

Is this your heart-felt desire? Do you desire, more than anything else, to love God and live according to His commandments? Do you hate sin? Those whose sins are forgiven by God also strive to live without sin. Do your sins bother you? Do you need God not ony to forgive your sins, but also to wash you clean from them?

MEMORIZATION QUESTIONS

1. What does God will that we should desire?
   Him only. Psalm 73:25

2. May we then not desire any food or drink?
   Yes, but that they may serve to direct us to God. I Corinthians 10:31

3. What is it to have food and drink serve to direct us to God?
   It is to acknowledge Him to be the giver of them. I Timothy 6:7

4. Why does God give us food and drink?
   In order that we may serve Him. Deuteronomy 8:10,11

5. What must we be mostly concerned about?
   Whether we have received the forgiveness of sins by the blood of Jesus Christ. Hebrews 9:22

6. Of what does the greatest good consist?
   Of knowing God and loving Him. Ecclesiastes 12:13

7. What must we fear the most?
   Sin. Genesis 39:9

8. Who can be comforted in death?
   Converted adults and children. Revelation 14:13

9. What must we forsake first?
   The world and the lusts thereof. I John 2:17

10. May children run the streets or associate with other naughty children?
    No, for though I am just as corrupt, I should learn more evil there. I Corinthians 15:33

11. What do children learn in the street?
    Swearing and speaking filthy language.

12. What has the Lord said about those who swear?
    That He will not hold him guiltless who taketh His name in vain.

13. What does that mean?
    That He will visit them with the very greatest punishments in both soul and body in hell.

    — Ledeboer's Catechism:
    Q. 34-37; 67-70; 85-89

CHAPTER CHECK-UP

1. Why are all people guilty and in debt to God?

   _____

   _____

2. Why do God's people not receive the punishment which their sins deserve?
   Who steps in between? Explain. _____

   _____

   _____

3. What are the two parts of justification?

   a. _____

   _____

   b. _____

   _____

4. On what ground or basis can a sinner be justified?_____

   _____

   _____

5. How can we be connected to the Lord Jesus Christ and His wonderful salvation? _____

   _____

   _____

6. In the history of the Passover, what is pictured and taught by:

   a. The lamb being without blemish? _____

   _____

b. The lamb being killed? _____

_____

c. The children of Israel who were standing behind the blood, being spared when God's judgment came? _____

_____

_____

7. What does the word "sanctify" mean? _____

_____

8. Name the two parts of sanctification:

a. _____

b. _____

9. God turning a person's heart from a deep love of sin to God is called _____. Walking according to God's commandments as a fruit of this turning is called _____.

10. a. Who works sanctification in the hearts of God's children?_____

b. What are some means of grace which the Holy Spirit blesses and we are commanded to use? _____

_____

c. Name some sinful means which we are not to use: _____

_____

11. Sanctification shows itself in _____ in a converted person's life.

PRAYER

PRAYER

Prayer is **communion** or speaking with God. Each of us should pray to God for all our needs. These needs must agree with God's will. We should also confess our sins to God and thank Him in prayer for all His blessings. Our prayers must be in the name of, and for the sake of, Jesus Christ.

True prayer was easy for Adam in Paradise. It was natural for him. Adam walked with God; they communed with one another. How sad that it did not remain this way.

> The Shorter Catechism says:
>
> "What is prayer? Prayer is an offering up of our desires unto God, for things agreeable to His will, in the name of Christ, with confession of our sins, and thankful acknowledgment of His mercies."

True prayer is different from only speaking some words. All of us pray outwardly, but possibly not all of us truly pray. Since our deep fall in Paradise, we serve ourselves and seek our own honor instead of God's honor. We now need the Holy Spirit to work true prayer in our hearts.

WHAT DO YOU THINK?

HONEST IN PRAYER

A man visited an elementary school one morning. He noticed the sad face of a boy who was usually cheerful. "Why are you so sad this morning?" he asked the boy.

Jim turned his face to hide his tears. His brother answered for him. "Mother is very angry with him because he would not say his prayers last night. Also, he cried all day yesterday. His pet sparrow, which he liked so much, died."

Jim then turned quickly and exclaimed, "I could not say, 'Thy will be done.' Why did my poor bird have to die?"

The man took Jim's hand and spoke to the class. "What Jim just said teaches us a lesson about prayer. How many of you only repeat the words of a prayer but do not really think about what you say?"

He then turned to Jim and said, "I am glad to hear that you were afraid to say to God that which you could not truly say from your heart. However, you must beg Him to give you submission to His will."

What part of true prayer is spoken about in this story?

— Adapted from *The NRC Banner of Truth*

True prayer includes the following elements:

ELEMENTS OF TRUE PRAYER	
1. FAITH A believing and trusting in God	**James 1:6** But let him ask *in faith*, nothing wavering. For he that wavereth is like a wave of the sea driven with the wind and tossed.
Revelation 15:4 Who shall not *fear Thee*, O Lord, and glorify Thy name? for *Thou only art holy:* for all nations shall come and worship before Thee; for Thy judgments are made manifest.	**2. REVERENCE** A deep respect for and worshipping of God
3. SUBMISSION A surrendering to God's will	**Luke 22:42** Saying, Father, if thou be willing, remove this cup from Me: nevertheless *not My will, but Thine, be done.*
Daniel 9:5 *We have sinned,* and have committed iniquity, and have done wickedly, and have rebelled, even, by departing from Thy precepts and from Thy judgments:	**4. REPENTANCE** A confession of and turning away from sin
5. SINCERITY A truthfulness from the heart	**Psalm 17:1** Hear the right, O LORD, attend unto my cry, give ear unto my prayer, that goeth *not out of feigned lips.*
Luke 18:3-5 And there was a widow in that city; and she came unto him, saying, Avenge me of mine adversary. And he would not for a while: but afterward he said within himself, Though I fear not God, nor regard man; Yet because this widow troubleth me, I will avenge her, lest by her *continual coming* she weary me.	**6. URGENCY** A felt need and concern which cannot be delayed

The Holy Spirit works true prayer in the hearts of people. We must pray with *faith.* We must believe and trust in God who answers prayer. True prayer is worshipping and honoring God with *reverence.* We must be *submissive* to God in prayer. "Thy will be done" must come before our own will. True prayer includes *repentance* and confession of our unworthiness. True prayer must be *sincere* and *urgent.* We must feel our need and look for an answer to our prayers.

Only God's people **can** truly pray through the work of the Holy Spirit. Yet all people **must** pray.

> Likewise the Spirit also helpeth our infirmities: for we know not what we should pray for as we ought: but **the Spirit itself maketh intercession for us** with groanings which cannot be uttered.
> — Romans 8:26

We are all commanded to pray. God's judgment is pronounced upon those who do not.

> **Seek ye the LORD** while He may be found, **call ye upon Him** while He is near.
> — Isaiah 55:6

> **Pour out Thy fury** upon the heathen that know Thee not and **upon the families that call not on Thy name.**
> — Jeremiah 10:25a

> And He spake a parable unto them to this end, **that men ought always to pray,** and not to faint.
> — Luke 18:1

WHAT DO YOU THINK?

A SHORT BUT MEANINGFUL PRAYER

George went to visit some friends who lived quite far from his home. On the way, he met a man who asked him, "Do you ever pray?"

"Yes, Sir!" answered George.

"And what do you pray?" asked the man.

"I say the prayer which my catechism teacher taught me, 'Lord, seek me first, and then I will seek Thee!'"

Is this a good prayer for unconverted people to pray? Why or why not?

— Adapted from *The NRC Banner of Truth*

For what must an unconverted person pray? We must all ask God to work in our hearts with His Spirit. Only then will we call upon His name in **uprightness** and truth. We must ask God to work in us that which we are missing. God commands us to ask Him for what we need. This command also includes children. Read the texts below. How do these verses encourage children to seek the Lord?

> And those that **seek Me early** shall find Me.
> — Proverbs 8:17b

> But Jesus said, Suffer **little children,** and forbid them not, to come unto Me: for of such is the kingdom of heaven.
> — Matthew 19:14

> For the promise is unto you, and to **your children,** and to all that are afar off, even as many as the Lord our God shall call.
> — Acts 2:39

Our prayers must be directed to God alone. We may neither worship nor pray to saints or angels. Read Revelation 19:10. When the Apostle John fell at the feet of the angel, what did the angel tell him? Whom must John worship instead of the angel?

For what must we pray? We must pray for all things necessary for soul and body, for ourselves and others. We must pray for all things necessary for our life here and the life to come. The most famous of all prayers teaches this. It shows us that for which we must pray. This prayer is called "The Lord's Prayer." It is named this because it was a prayer given by the Lord Jesus Himself. He spoke this prayer to His disciples when they asked Him to teach them how to pray. Read this prayer carefully. Do you know this prayer?

In what posture or position must we pray? The *position* of our body should show humbleness and reverence for God. How can humbleness and respect be seen in the postures of Solomon, Elijah, and the publican when they prayed?

> And I fell at his feet to **worship him.** And he said unto me, See thou **do it not:** I am thy fellowservant, and of thy brethren that have the testimony of Jesus: **worship God:** for the testimony of Jesus is the spirit of prophecy.
> — Revelation 19:10

> And as Peter was coming in, Cornelius met him, and fell down at his feet, and **worshipped** him.
> But Peter took him up saying, **Stand up;** I myself also am a man.
> — Acts 10:25-26

WHAT DO YOU THINK?

THE LORD'S PRAYER

After this manner therefore pray ye: Our Father which art in heaven, Hallowed be Thy name.

Thy kingdom come. Thy will be done in earth, as it is in heaven.

Give us this day our daily bread.

And forgive us our debts, as we forgive our debtors.

And lead us not into temptation, but deliver us from evil: For Thine is the kingdom, and the power, and the glory, for ever. Amen.

Matthew 6:9-13

Which parts of this prayer ask for: the honoring of God's name, the supplying of our bodily needs, and the forgiveness of our sins? Where can you see expressions of faith, reverence, repentance, and submission in this prayer?

WHAT DO YOU THINK?

SOLOMON

And kneeled down **upon his knees** before all the congregation of Israel, and spread forth his hands toward heaven.
— II Chronicles 6:13b

ELIJAH

And Elijah went up to the top of Carmel; and he **cast himself down upon the earth,** and **put his face between his knees.**
— I Kings 18:42b

PUBLICAN

And the publican, standing afar off, would **not lift up so much as his eyes unto heaven,** but smote upon his breast, saying, God be merciful to me a sinner.
— Luke 18:13

How do these postures show humbleness and reverence when praying?

When we pray, we close our eyes and fold our hands. We close our eyes to close out the things of this world. We must pray to God who is a Spirit. We may not expect our help from things we see, but from God. We fold our hands to show that we must not trust in our own strength or work; we must submit to God. We need His help and care. We need to stand, sit, or kneel properly. This shows humbleness and respect. If you came into the presence of an earthly king and were allowed to speak to him, wouldn't you try to do this as respectfully as possible? How much more concerned you should be when you speak with the King of kings, God Himself!

The Bible mentions some set times for prayer each day. Read the following texts. What times are mentioned? Do you have set times for your own private prayer each day?

My voice shalt Thou hear in the **morning,** O LORD; in the morning will I direct my prayer unto Thee, and will look up.
— Psalm 5:3

And He commanded the multitude to sit down on the grass, and took the five loaves, and the two fishes, and looking up to heaven, **He blessed,** and brake, **and gave the loaves to His disciples,** and the disciples to the multitude.
— Matthew 14:19

Now when Daniel knew that the writing was signed, he went into his house; and his windows being open in his chamber toward Jerusalem, he kneeled upon his knees **three times a day,** and prayed, and gave thanks before His God, as he did aforetime.
— Daniel 6:10

When **thou hast eaten** and art full, **then thou shalt bless the LORD** thy God for the good land which He hath given thee.
— Deuteronomy 8:10

There are special times for prayer, but we should be of a prayerful spirit all the time. There are always many reasons for prayer no matter where you are. How did the chimney sweep find time to pray? When do you pray?

WHAT DO YOU THINK?

THE LITTLE CHIMNEY SWEEP'S PRAYER

The children in my Sunday School class had to work hard during the week. I was afraid that they were sometimes forgetting to pray. Therefore, I spoke one Sunday about the importance of prayer. Ten-year-old Peter had to work very hard as a chimney sweep. I asked him, "Peter, do you ever pray?"

"Oh yes, Sir!" he replied.

"And when do you do this? You go out very early in the morning, don't you?"

"Yes, Sir, and we are only half awake when we leave the house. I think about God, but I cannot say that I pray then."

"When then?"

"You see, Sir, our master orders us to climb the chimney quickly, but we are allowed to rest a little when we are at the top. Then I sit on the chimney top and pray."

"And what do you pray?"

"Ah, Sir, very little. I don't know any beautiful words with which to speak to God. Usually I only repeat a verse that I have learned at school."

"What is that?"

Peter answered very earnestly, "God be merciful to me a sinner."

Do you find time during your day to pray as this young chimney sweep did? Do prayers need to be long to be sincere?

— Adapted from **The NRC Banner of Truth**

AS GRANDFATHER DOES

Jacob and Anna lived with their little boy, John, in the German village of Berheim. John was blessed with a God-fearing grandfather who had prayed for him ever since he was born. When he was baptized, Grandfather had chosen the name "John" for him saying, "May he be loved by God in time and throughout all eternity."

Grandfather often came to visit little John. Many times he would lay his hand on John's head and say, "The Lord bless you, my child; the Lord bless you and keep you as the apple of His eye." Grandfather's prayers were not left unanswered.

On Grandfather's sixtieth birthday, John went with his parents to see him. John was very happy to spend the whole day with his grandfather. His father had to go back home for the day, but promised to return that evening. However, a terrible thunderstorm came up which made it impossible for him to return. Therefore, John and his mother had to spend the night at Grandfather's house. Little John was delighted, but his mother did not feel at ease in Grandfather's presence.

When evening came, everyone gathered together. John's grandfather opened his large Bible and read a chapter. He then offered up an earnest and child-like prayer out of the fulness of his heart. He especially remembered his birthday. Everyone then went to bed.

The following morning, Anna left to walk back with her child. It was a lovely summer day, and the walk through the woods and past several little waterfalls was very pleasant. John loved flowers and seldom walked past them. But today he walked behind his mother as seriously and quietly as though there was not a single flower to be seen. Anna did not feel much like talking either. Her mind was uneasy, but she did not know why.

All of a sudden, John stood still, looked up into his mother's face, and asked, "Mother, why doesn't Father do as Grandfather does?"

His mother became somewhat confused. "Go and look for flowers," she said, and walked on.

So they went on silently, but John was not thinking about flowers. Soon they came to the top of a hill, where there was a beautiful view of the distant mountains. Anna sat down to rest for a while, and John sat beside her. "Mother," he said for the second time, "why doesn't Father do as Grandfather does?"

Anna felt impatient. "Well," she answered rather sharply, "and what does Grandfather do?"

"He takes the large Bible," said John, "and he reads and prays."

His mother blushed. "You must ask your father about it," she answered.

When they reached home, Father was not there. He had gone to harvest in a field quite far away and would not be back until evening. John's mother knew this and thought she would put her boy to bed early. She hoped that by morning he would have forgotten his question.

But, she was mistaken. As she was going to undress him, he said, "No, Mother; just let me wait until Father comes home."

At eight o'clock, his father returned. John ran up to him directly and asked, "Father, why don't you do as Grandfather does?"

His father looked hard at him. The question came unexpectedly. "What are you doing up yet, John?" he asked. "Go to bed now; it's late."

John was silent, but went sorrowfully to bed. He got up the next morning with still more sadness. He was a different child from what he usually was. He sat silently and sadly at the breakfast table, with his hands folded and head down. He had not touched his milk. "What is the matter, John? Why don't you eat?" asked his mother.

John was silent.

After a little while she asked again, "What is it, child?" He looked up at his mother very sadly for a moment and bowed his head again. His father and mother had finished, and were going to clear the breakfast table. His mother asked a third time, "Child, tell me what is the matter."

Then the boy answered, "I want so much to pray, Mother; but no one will pray with me. I must pray alone."

This was too much for Anna. Tears filled her eyes. She hurried into the next room to tell her husband what the child had said. He had heard, however, what John had said, for the door was left open. His conscience was touched. "John is right," he said, "and we are wrong." Then they fell on their knees together for the first time in their married life. They prayed a prayer with few words but with many tears. It was the publican's prayer: "God be merciful to us, sinners!"

The happy day had arrived when little John no longer had to pray alone. Father and Mother now began to bend their knees together before the Lord to ask for His mercy and forgiveness. They asked for a new heart and for grace for themselves and their child to live entirely for Him.

Do you love to pray as John did? Are you thankful for, and attentive during, family prayer at home?

— Adapted from *The NRC Banner of Truth*

SOME PRAYERS FOR CHILDREN

Before Meals

Lord, bless this food and drink unto my body and Thy Word unto my soul, for Jesus' sake.

Amen

Lord, bless this food, and grant that we
May thankful for Thy mercies be;
Teach us to know by whom we're fed,
Bless us with Christ, the living Bread.

Amen

After Meals

Lord, I thank Thee for this food and drink. Above all I thank Thee for Thy Word. Please bless them to my body and soul for Jesus' sake.

Amen

Most merciful God; Thy name be praised and thanked for all these loving gifts Thou hast so graciously bestowed upon us again. Wilt Thou further feed our souls with the Bread of Life, and strengthen our hearts through Thy grace, that our life and death might be to the glory and honor of Thy most holy Name.

Amen

O Lord, with heartfelt thanks we come to Thee, to acknowledge Thee for the abundance of this life's necessities. While many eat their bread in grief and sorrow, Thou hast fed us kindly in an abundant measure. Oh, grant that our souls may not cleave to the things of this perishing world, that our life may be in the path of Thy commandments, and in the end have everlasting life with Thee.

Amen

In the Morning

Lord, I thank Thee for this day,
Guide and lead me in Thy way.
Teach me, Lord, Thy truth to know
That in Thy path I may go.

Amen

Now I wake to see the light,
'Tis God who kept me through the night.
And now I lift my voice to pray,
That God will keep me through the day.

Amen

In the Evening

Now I lay me down to sleep,
I pray Thee, Lord, my soul to keep.
If I should die before I wake
I pray Thee, Lord, my soul to take.
If I should live for other days,
I pray Thee, Lord, to guide my ways.

Amen

MEMORIZATION QUESTIONS

1. What must happen to us, shall we enter heaven?
   The Lord Jesus must come and take up His abode in our hearts. II Corinthians 13:5

2. Must we pray to Him for this?
   Yes, because He has said, "Seek ye the Lord while He may be found, call ye upon Him while He is near." Isaiah 55:6

3. Will it do to wait till we have become old?
   No, because I am not assured of my life for one moment. Hebrews 4:7

4. What is the chief good work?
   Prayer.

5. Whom ought we to worship?
   God alone. Matthew 4:10

6. Why ought we not to worship the saints?
   Because this honor does not belong to them. Revelation 19:10

7. How ought we to pray?
   "Our Father, which art in heaven," etc. Matthew 6:9-13

8. What does Christ say about the children?
   Suffer little children, and forbid them not, to come unto Me: for of such is the kingdom of heaven. Matthew 19:14

— Ledeboer's Catechism Q. 60-62
— Borstius Catechism: Lesson XXVII, Q. 1-5

CHAPTER CHECK-UP

1. What is prayer? _____
   _____
   _____

2. Name six things (elements) found in true prayer and explain what each means:

   a. _____ — _____
   _____

   b. _____ — _____
   _____

   c. _____ — _____
   _____

   d. _____ — _____
   _____

   e. _____ — _____
   _____

   f. _____ — _____
   _____

3. a. Must an unconverted person pray? _____

   b. For what must he pray? _____
   _____
   _____

4. Write out the last part of Proverbs 8:17 — _____
   _____
   _____

CHAPTER CHECK-UP

5. To whom must we pray? _____

6. For what must we pray? (Answer fully and carefully)

   _____

   _____

   _____

7. What is the name of the prayer which Jesus taught His disciples to pray in

   Matthew 6:9-13? _____

8. When we pray:

   a. Why do we close our eyes? _____

   _____

   b. Why do we fold our hands? _____

   _____

9. In the story, **As Grandfather Does**, why was John so sad after he left his grand-

   father's house?

   _____

   _____

   _____

10. Name some "set times" for prayer spoken of in the Bible:

    a. _____

    b. _____

    c. _____

    d. _____

REVIEW QUESTIONS

1. a. After our deep fall in Paradise, is there any hope for salvation *in man?* ____

   Why not? _____

   _____

   b. Is there any hope for salvation *in God?* _____ Why? _____

   _____

   _____

2. Who suffered the full punishment for the sins of God's people?

   _____

3. The two parts of justification are:

   a. _____

   b. _____

4. How can we be connected to the Lord Jesus Christ? _____

   _____

5. The two parts of sanctification are:

   a. _____

   b. _____

6. Name the two fighting sides in the spiritual war within the heart of a converted

   person.

   a. _____

   b. _____

7. Who works sanctification in the hearts of God's children?

   _____

8.   Name six things found in true prayer:

a.   _____   d.   _____

b.   _____   e.   _____

c.   _____   f.   _____

9.   For what must an unconverted person pray? _____

_____

_____

10. Why was true prayer natural and easy for Adam in Paradise? _____

_____

11. We must pray for all things which are necessary for both _____ and

_____, for ourselves and for _____

12. Our position or posture in prayer should show _____ and

_____

13. When we pray, why do we:

a.   Close our eyes? _____

_____

b.   Fold our hands? _____

_____

14. a.   Does the Bible mention "set times" for prayer during the day?_____

b.   Give some Biblical examples of "set times" for prayer: _____

_____

_____

WORD SEARCH

```
G A G P B U O N O I S S I M B U S C I S L
T U I J J T I O N U C A R Y P G O E C N S
I L I L U O N T I F E N E B T U L L O P S
F S N L S S E N T E N C E V E D I E M F E
S U B S T I T U T E E T N R D E S U M N N
G E V P I E A I R R A I N A C D I E U I I
S S C E C R Y N F D E F E N D I N G N W H
O I R N E T P O S I T I O N H D C I I N T
E D S Y E G N I S U C C A S E S E A O N R
C A A T I R G O I N C A U B T S R I N B O
S R T O R I E N T C I T T O N U I W C D W
P A F G U H J V I L P I J I R W T E Y P N
U P R I G H T N E S S O C S O A Y T O N U
E C N A T N E P E R P N S Y C N E G R U A
```

Find and circle each of the twenty NEW WORDS found in Chapters 13 and 14.
Write the correct word next to its meaning.

_____ The act of having friendship

_____ Blaming someone for wrongdoing

_____ To help another

_____ Obedience; the act of surrendering

_____ The being washed from the pollution of sin

_____ That which is important and cannot be delayed

_____ Innocency

_____ The fact of having broken a law

_____ Posture of the body

_____ Fairness; a just punishment

_____ A true sorrowing for and fleeing from sin

_____ The forgiveness of the guilt of sin

_____ One who takes the place of another

_____ Honesty; truthfulness

_____ Protecting another

_____ An attitude of deep respect

_____ The act of earnestly asking and thanking God for our needs and blessings

_____ That which is owed and must be paid

_____ The condition of being undeserving

_____ The pronouncement of a guilty person's punishment by a judge

BIBLE STUDY QUESTIONS

Draw a line to connect each doctrinal truth with the text which most clearly teaches this truth.

DOCTRINAL TRUTHS

1. God's children are justified by faith in Jesus Christ and not by their own works.

2. Our duty is to love God and to keep His commandments.

3. All people are commanded to pray.

4. We must pray that God's will would be done above our own wills.

5. We must pray in faith.

6. We should pray be,ore a meal.

7. We should pray after a meal.

TEXTS

A.   Ecclesiastes 12:13

Let us hear the conclusion of the whole matter: Fear God, and keep His commandments: for this is the whole duty of man.

B.   Luke 22:42

Saying, Father, if Thou be willing, remove this cup from Me: nevertheless not My will, but Thine, be done.

C.   Matthew 14:19

And He commanded the multitude to sit down on the grass, and took the five loaves, and the two fishes, and looking up to heaven, He blessed, and brake, and gave the loaves to His disciples, and the disciples to the multitude.

D.   Romans 5:1

Therefore being justified by faith, we have peace with God through our Lord Jesus Christ.

E.   Deuteronomy 8:10

When thou hast eaten and art full, then thou shalt bless the LORD thy God for the good land which He hath given thee.

F.   Isaiah 55:6

Seek ye the LORD while He may be found, call ye upon Him while He is near.

G.   James 1:6

But let him ask in faith, nothing wavering. For he that wavereth is like a wave of the sea driven with the wind and tossed.

CHAPTER 15

THE CHURCH
THE CHURCH OFFICES

THE CHURCH

When the Bible speaks of the **church,** it does not mean a building. The true meaning of the word "church" is "all true believers in Christ" (all those who are God's children).

The Lord Jesus Christ is pictured in God's Word as the Head of His church. His people are pictured as His body because they are so closely **united** to Him.

> For the husband is the head of the wife, even as **Christ is the head of the church:** and He is the Savior of the body.
> — Ephesians 5:23

The church is both visible and invisible. It is both seen and unseen.

WHAT DO YOU THINK?

THE CHURCH

What is the meaning of the word "church" in these verses from Acts?

> And when they were come to Jerusalem, they were received of the **church** and of the apostles and elders, and they declared all things that God had done with them. — Acts 15:4

> Then had the **churches** rest throughout all Judea and Galilee and Samaria. — Acts 9:31a

> And great fear came upon all the **church,** and upon as many as heard these things. — Acts 5:11

> Take heed therefore unto yourselves, and to all the flock, over the which the Holy Ghost hath made you overseers, to feed the **Church** of God, which He hath purchased with His own blood. — Acts 20:28

WHAT DO YOU THINK?

![church illustration]

LIGHT FROM ABOVE

A man visited a famous old church building. There was a very low, thick fog that morning. He could hardly find the church. With difficulty he finally found the door and went inside.

He stood there amazed. A bright circle of sunlight lit up the front of the church! How could this be when it was so foggy outside?

Suddenly he saw the answer. The light came through the top windows of a high tower in the church. The top of this tower was above the low-hanging fog!

Seeing this light taught the man a beautiful lesson. How is this example true spiritually? How is the spiritual light which shines in the church above the spiritual darkness here below?

— Adapted from *3,000 Illustrations for Christian Service*

After this I beheld, and, lo, *a great multitude,* which no man could number, *of all nations, and kindreds, and people, and tongues,* stood before the throne, and before the Lamb, clothed with white robes, and palms in their hands:
— Revelation 7:9

This can be explained as follows:

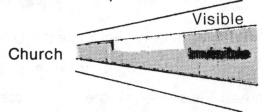

The **Church Visible** is all people who join together to worship God. We can see these people gathering together each Sunday under the Word of God.

The **Church Invisible** is all true believers. They have been converted from loving sin to loving God. Christ is their Head and they are His body. They have received true saving faith. The true believers are invisible to us. We cannot see exactly who is saved or who is not. But each is clearly known and seen by God.

For he is not a Jew, which is one *outwardly;* neither is that circumcision, which is outward in the flesh:
But he is a Jew, which is one *inwardly,* and circumcision is that of the heart, in the spirit, and not in the letter; whose praise is not of men, but of God.
— Romans 2:28-29

For they are *not all Israel, which are of Israel.*
— Romans 9:6b

They answered and said unto Him, Abraham is our father. Jesus saith unto them, If ye were *Abraham's children,* ye would *do the works of Abraham.*
— John 8:39

The Church Invisible will be found and gathered from all over the world. No one church **denomination** will have all of God's true children. They can be found in many different church denominations. Also, no church denomination will have only true believers as members. Read the Parable of the Tares. What is meant by the **tares** (or weeds) growing with the wheat in the same field until harvest?

The Church Invisible has two parts: the **Church Militant** and the **Church Triumphant.** This can be pictured in the following way:

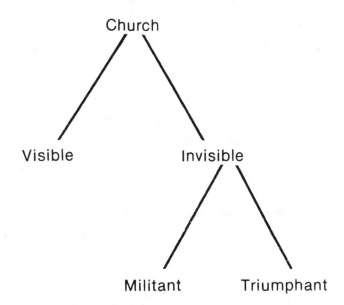

The **Church Militant** is the Church Invisible **on earth**. "Militant" means "fighting in a war or conflict." God's children are fighting a spiritual war as long as they live on earth. They are fighting against powerful enemies. They are at war with Satan, sin, world, and their sinful selves. A true believer's new nature which strives to love God is at war with his old nature which loves sin. Furthermore, the forces of Satan are at war with the forces of God in the world.

While the enemies of the Church Militant are very strong, yet God's children shall gain the victory in the end. This is not because of their own strength or faithfulness. They will gain the victory through Jesus Christ who is their Head and Captain. He has gained the victory over their enemies for them.

WHAT DO YOU THINK?

THE PARABLE OF THE TARES

Matthew 13:24-30

Another parable put He forth unto them, saying, The kingdom of heaven is likened unto a man which sowed good seed in his field:

But while men slept, his enemy came and sowed tares among the wheat, and went his way.

But when the blade was sprung up, and brought forth fruit, then appeared the tares also.

So the servants of the householder came and said unto him, Sir, didst not thou sow good seed in thy field? from whence then hath it tares?

He said unto them, An enemy hath done this. The servants said unto him, Wilt thou then that we go and gather them up?

But he said, Nay; llest while ye gather up the tares, ye root up also the wheat with them.

Let both grow together until the harvest: and in the time of harvest I will say to the reapers, Gather ye together first the tares, and bind them in bundles to burn them: but gather the wheat into my barn.

What is pictured in this parable by:
— The wheat?
— The tares?
— The field?
— The owner of the field?
— The owner's servants?
— The enemy who sowed the tares?
— The wheat and tares growing together?
— The harvest?
— The tares being burned?
— The wheat being gathered into the barn?

Why was the servant forbidden to pull out the tares before the harvest? How is this a picture of the Church Visible and the Church Invisible?

When a true soldier in this spiritual war dies, then he is taken into heaven. There he will join all other true believers. In heaven, they shall celebrate their victory over sinful self, sin, world, and Satan through Christ their Head. For this reason, the church *in heaven* is called the **Church Triumphant.**

After the final Judgment Day, the entire Church Invisible will be triumphant. Then all God's children will be brought into heaven with both soul and body. There they shall rejoice over their spiritual enemies who are cast away forever. They will then praise, honor, glorify, and rejoice in God forever for His wonderful deliverance and victory.

AN AWFUL JUDGMENT FOR MOCKING IN CHURCH

Rev. Fleming, a godly minister, was preaching in Amsterdam, a city in The Netherlands. During his sermon, three boys began to misbehave in the back of the church. It became necessary for Rev. Fleming to stop and speak to the boys from the pulpit. But this seemed to make the boys' behavior worse instead of better. Rev. Fleming had to stop a second time to warn them. But their mocking and laughing still grew louder.

In the middle of the sermon, the minister stopped for the third time. Trembling with grief and emotion, he looked at the boys and said, "My young friends, it hurts me very much, but I must give each of you an awful message! I begged the Lord to change it, but He will not. Each of you has less than one week to live."

A stunned silence fell over the entire congregation. The minister could hardly continue. Everyone was talking about this after church.

All three boys died in that week. On Tuesday, one boy died in a boat accident; on Wednesday, the second was killed in a fight; and on Thursday, the third became seriously ill. He called Rev. Fleming to please come and pray with him for forgiveness, which Rev. Fleming did. The following day, he too, died.

This awful lesson shows how important a church service is! We may never mock in God's house. We must always try to listen carefully and respectfully. How does this story show the truths of Galatians 6:7 in a powerful way?

— Adapted from *Religious Stories for Young and Old*

When we attend a church service, we must do so seriously, reverently, and prayerfully. The preaching of God's Word is an important means of grace. God will bless the preaching of His Word to convert sinners and to strengthen and comfort His true children. God is present in a special way during a church service. The church is called "God's House." Therefore, we must never attend church carelessly.

WHAT DO YOU THINK?

HOW DO YOU GO TO CHURCH?

An older man once said, "When I was young, I used to think that church was a place where you *had* to go, even though it was quite boring. However, I always saw how interested my father and mother were. They were going to church because they *wanted* to, not because they *had* to.

This made me feel that my parents found something in church that I was missing. This left more of an impression upon me of the value of church and spiritual things than anything else when I was a boy."

How do you go to church? Do you go because you *have* to, or because you *want* to? Are you more interested in spiritual truths or in worldly things?

A COSTLY SLEEP!

Sally lived in a large apartment building in a big city. Behind her apartment house was a little piece of land where her family had a small garden. One morning Sally's mother sent her out to weed their garden.

However, Sally did not like to pull weeds. So she went behind some bushes at the side of the garden and lay back on the grass. She watched the clouds moving in the sky and dreamed of her eleventh birthday. Soon she grew tired and fell fast asleep.

Her Uncle Bob made a surprise visit to Sally's apartment. He was returning from a business trip and was on his way back to his farm which was about 300 miles away. "I need to leave right away," said Uncle Bob to Sally's mother, "but I am wondering, would Sally like to come and spend a week with us at the farm? I have to return in a week and this would be a nice opportunity for her."

"Oh, she would just love that!" her mother exclaimed, "I'll call her right away!"

But no Sally answered when Mother called. Her mother could not find her anywhere! After searching for half an hour, Uncle Bob had to leave without her.

Poor Sally! How she cried when she found out! "Why did I have to sleep? Why?" she kept sobbing to herself. "I never heard Mother call because I was fast asleep."

This certainly was a costly sleep, wasn't it?

In church, a more valuable offer is being made than a visit to a farm for one week. God is offering salvation to sinners through Jesus Christ. Yet sometimes there are people sleeping! They do not hear God's call. If they would die in this way, why would their sleeping be most costly? How is your behavior in church? Do you try to listen carefully?

CHURCH OFFICES

The Lord Jesus is Head and King of His Church. He has given three offices and three types of *officebearers* to lead and rule the church according to His Word. The three types of officebearers are:

1. Ministers
2. Elders
3. Deacons

MINISTERS

Who then is Paul, and who is Apollos, but *ministers* by whom ye believed, even as the Lord gave to every man?
— I Corinthians 3:5

ELDERS

Let the *elders* that rule well be counted worthy of double honour, especially they who labour in the word and doctrine.
— I Timothy 5:17

DEACONS

And let these also first be proved; then let them use the office of a *deacon*, being found blameless.
— I Timothy 3:10

Each of these three offices has separate duties.

The office of a *Minister* includes:

1. Preaching the Word of God
2. Administering baptism and the Lord's supper
3. Praying for the congregation
4. Helping govern the church with the elders
5. Visiting the sick, teaching the youth, and warning and comforting the families in the congregation.

The office of an *Elder* includes:

1. Ruling and governing the church with the minister.
2. Upholding and guarding the true doctrines of God's Word in the teachings of the church and in the lives of the members.
3. Helping the minister in giving instruction, advice, and comfort to the families of the congregation.
4. Leading church services if the minister is absent or if there is no minister in the congregation.

The office of a *Deacon* includes:

1. Receiving the gifts given to the church and caring for the proper spending of the money collected.
2. Visiting and caring for the poor, both materially and spiritually.

There were also three offices in the Old Testament church. Can you see how those offices and their duties compare to the New Testament offices? This is shown on the following chart:

OLD TESTAMENT OFFICE	MAIN DUTY	NEW TESTAMENT OFFICE
PROPHET	To teach and preach God's Word	MINISTER
PRIEST	To receive and offer the gifts of the people	DEACON
KING	To rule and govern	ELDER

It is our duty to respect the church office bearers for God has placed them in their offices.

WHAT DO YOU THINK?

RESPECT GOD'S OFFICEBEARERS

There is a Bible story which clearly warns us never to mock or laugh at God's office-bearers.

After Elijah was taken up into heaven, Elisha took his place on earth as God's prophet to the children of Israel. One day as he was walking to Bethel, some children followed him yelling, "Go up, thou bald head! Go up, thou bald head!" They mocked Elijah's going up into heaven and Elisha's baldness.

Do you know what happened? God punished them most severely. Two bears came out of the woods and killed forty-two of the children! Never mock God's office-bearers, but respect them. Can you see from this story how God punished those who mocked His servants?

WHAT DO YOU THINK?

A TRUE MINISTER

Rev. Hans Egede felt that God had called him to preach His Word to the heathen Eskimos that lived in Greenland. This was not possible for some years, but finally God opened a way. Rev. Egede arrived with a Danish trading company in 1721.

At that time the Eskimos in Greenland had never heard about the true God or His Word. They were a very fierce people. If a ship was blown to their shore in a storm, they often killed the people and took all the goods on the ship. A human life was not worth much to them.

This is where Rev. Egede landed. He first built a little hut of dirt, stones, and boards in this very cold country for his family. He then tried to learn the Eskimo language. He visited the people in their igloos which were heated by burning whale oil. The smell was almost unbearable for Rev. Egede, but he continued. He tried to speak to them about God, sin, and salvation in Jesus Christ, but the people only laughed at him.

The trading company decided that they could not work with these people. They told Rev. Egede to pack his things for they were leaving. Rev. Egede had now worked there for two years, but no one was listening to him. Shouldn't he leave? He should. . . but he could not. He stayed behind alone with his family.

More years went by and still there were no fruits upon his preaching. Then a plague of smallpox broke out. Several Eskimos died from this serious disease. Smallpox is so contagious that no one dared to enter an igloo where someone had the disease. However, Rev. Egede visited, spoke to, and tried to help each sick person. This made a deep impression upon the Eskimos. They began to see that it must be an important message which Rev. Egede was bringing. He must be a wonderful man to risk his life for others in this way. After the plague, a few Eskimos started coming to hear him. Then more and more came. God blessed his preaching and fruits of conversion were seen. Can you imagine Rev. Egede's joy after working there for so many years? He stayed with the Eskimos for a total of fifteen years and saw a complete change in the people.

Can you see in this story, the love and strong desire to bring God's Word which is found in a true minister's heart? Are you interested in God's message which your minister brings to you?

WHAT DO YOU THINK?

ANSWERED PRAYER

Sambo, an old Negro man, told the following story:

When I was a boy, my father and mother were slaves. My father was a good man. He was a member of the Methodist Church. There was a large family Bible with pictures in it in our cottage. My father often sat beside me in the evenings to show me the pictures and tell me all about them. One day he showed me a picture of Daniel in the lions' den and told me how Daniel had prayed to God. Then he said, "Now, Sambo, if you have Christ as your Savior, and Daniel's God as your God; if you ever get into danger, think of Daniel in the den of lions. Pray as he prayed, and God will protect you."

Later he sent me to the Mission school. I was taught to read, and before I was ten years old, I could read a little for myself.

When I became a teenager, I received my freedom, and was hired on a ship as an apprentice. My master came from London, and was a very kind man. The men on this ship were very kind to me. When they found that I could read a little, they gave me things to copy, and I learned to write. Then I could send letters to my father and tell him how I was getting along. I also had a Bible which I read. The men on the ship were not angry with me,

but they thought I was too religious. I did not make much of it. I just read the Book because my father had told me that it would make me happy.

When my training was over, I worked on another English ship. This captain was not a good man. He was rough and often swore. Because I was a good-looking black fellow, he took me into his cabin to serve him. Although he was a rough man, he was very kind-hearted and treated me well.

One night I was on watch. I was leaning over the rail when the ship suddenly tipped and I fell into the sea. Never shall I forget that awful moment! It was a very dark night and I was not missed. I could swim like a fish and floating in the water, I took off my boots, coat, and other heavy clothing. With sinking heart, I watched the back lights of our ship disappearing in the distance! I was not afraid of drowning. I was able to float in the water for twenty-four hours and would most likely be picked up by that time. But I was afraid of

sharks. They can smell a man in the water from miles away. What could I do now?

I remembered what my father had told me to do if I would ever be in danger. I thought of Daniel in the lions' den. I remembered how God had shut the mouths of the lions, and prayed to God that He would shut the mouths of the sharks! God heard my prayer. The sharks swam around me, but they did not harm me.

Finally, to my great joy, I heard the sound of oars. I had been missed when the watch was called, and a boat was sent out to search for me. They soon took me in. When I was back on the ship again, all my shipmates were amazed that I had not been eaten by sharks. I told them that the God who had protected Daniel in the lions' den had saved me.

How did God bless the instruction given to Sambo, when he was young, in his later life? Why is it a great blessing to be brought up in church and under its instruction when we are young?

— Adapted from *The NRC Banner of Truth*

MEMORIZATION WORK: I Corinthians 12:12-14, 26-28

CHAPTER CHECK-UP

1. a. What is the true meaning of the word "church"? _____

_____

_____

   b. What is a church denomination? _____

_____

_____

2. The two parts of the church are the Church _____ and the

Church _____.

3. a. What is the Church Visible? _____

_____

_____

   b. What is the Church Invisible? _____

_____

_____

4. What are the two parts of the Church Invisible and what does each part mean?

   a. The Church _____ — _____

_____

_____

   b. The Church _____ — _____

_____

_____

CHAPTER CHECK-UP

5. How must we attend church and why? _____

_____

_____

6. Name the three types of offices and officebearers in the New Testament Church:

   a. _____

   b. _____

   c. _____

7. What is the main duty of each office? (See the chart on page 63.)

   a. Minister — _____

   b. Elder — _____

   c. Deacon — _____

8. Match the three Old Testament offices with the three New Testament church offices by drawing a line to connect those which are similar.

Old Testament Office	*New Testament Church Office*
Prophet	Elder
Priest	Minister
King	Deacon

9. Why must we respect the church officebearers? _____

_____

_____

CHAPTER 16

**DOCTRINAL STANDARDS
CREEDS
THE FIVE POINTS OF CALVINISM**

DOCTRINAL STANDARDS

Doctrines are the truths of God's Word. Bible verses which speak about the same truths can be grouped together. Then **statements** can be written which clearly explain what the entire Bible is teaching about these truths. These statements of doctrine are called **Doctrinal Standards.** Each church denomination has doctrinal standards.

Doctrinal standards do not take the place of the Bible. Instead, they tell us what the entire Bible is teaching about a certain doctrine.

A standard is something which represents a group of people. A standard can be a sign, flag, official writing, or something else. A flag is the standard of a country. The flag of our country means something to us for we belong to this country. The flag reminds us that we are citizens

WHAT DO YOU THINK?

THE FLAG OF CANADA

This is the standard of Canada. All those who live in Canada recognize this standard and stand behind it.

Why does this flag have a special meaning to the citizens of Canada?

69

THAT'S OUR FLAG!

Imagine attending a world-wide conference. Thousands of people are there from many countries of the world.

When you come into the main area, there are so many people that you cannot find your way and become lost.

You walk all around trying to find someone from your country with whom you can speak, but you cannot find anyone you know. If you speak with strangers you do not know whether they will be able to understand you. You feel hopelessly lost!

Finally, you see your country's flag in the distance. How glad you are! You quickly work your way there through the crowd. Under your flag you find people from your own country. Now you feel at home and start talking with your fellow citizens.

How are doctrinal standards like a flag? What do the "citizens" under the same doctrinal standards have in common?

of this country

Doctrinal standards are clear writings about the doctrines which we believe. They have a special meaning for us as church members. They show and teach us where we stand. Doctrinal standards clearly explain what God is teaching about each truth throughout His Word.

Do you remember from Chapter One, what our three doctrinal standards are called? They are:

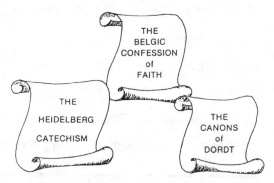

These three doctrinal standards are often called **The Three Forms of Unity.** They show the **unity** of those who believe in these explanations of the Bible. The Three Forms of Unity are the doctrinal standards of all Reformed churches.

CREEDS

Creeds are statements which often begin with the words "I believe. . ." Creeds are statements of belief with little or no explanation. We believe in three creeds. They are the:

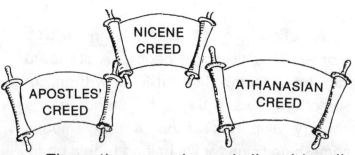

These three creeds are believed by all Christian churches.

OUR THREE DOCTRINAL STANDARDS

HEIDELBERG CATECHISM

The Heidelberg Catechism was written in 1562. It was written by Zacharias Ursinus, a professor of theology, and Casper Olevianus, a minister.

The Heidelberg Catechism has 129 questions and answers explaining Bible doctrines. It is divided into fifty-two Lord's Days. Why fifty-two, do you think?

Can you find this doctrinal standard in the back of your Psalter?

CONFESSION OF FAITH

The Confession of Faith was written by Guido de Brès, a minister, in the year 1561. He wrote it during a time of persecution. It was thrown over the castle wall for the king to find and read. Six years later, Guido de Brès died as a martyr.

The Confession of Faith has thirty-seven articles which explain the main doctrines.

Can you find this doctrinal standard in the back of your Psalter?

CANONS OF DORDT

The Canons of Dordt were written by the Synod of Dordt in 1618 and 1619. The chairman of this synod was Johannes Bogerman. This doctrinal standard is divided into five parts called the Five Heads of Doctrine. These five parts explain "The Five Points of Calvinism." You will read more about these five points in this chapter.

Can you find this doctrinal standard in the back of your Psalter?

THE THREE CREEDS OF ALL CHRISTIAN CHURCHES

APOSTLES' CREED

I.   I believe in God the Father, Almighty, Maker of heaven and earth:

II. And in Jesus Christ, His only begotten Son, our Lord:

III. Who was conceived by the Holy Ghost, born of the Virgin Mary:

IV. Suffered under Pontius Pilate; was crucified, dead, and buried: He descended into hell:

V.   The third day He rose again from the dead:

VI. He ascended into heaven, and sitteth at the right hand of God the Father Almighty:

VII. From thence He shall come to judge the quick and the dead:

/III. I believe in the Holy Ghost:

IX. I believe an holy catholic church: the communion of saints:

X.   The forgiveness of sins:

XI. The resurrection of the body:

XII. And the life everlasting. AMEN.

NICENE CREED

I believe in one God, the Father Almighty, Maker of heaven and earth, and of all things visible and invisible.

And in one Lord Jesus Christ, the only begotten Son of God, begotten of the Father before all worlds; God of God, Light of Light, very God of very God; begotten, not made, being of one substance with the Father, by Whom all things were made.

Who, for us men for our salvation, came down from heaven, and was incarnate by the Holy Spirit of the Virgin Mary, and was made man; and was crucified also for us under Pontius Pilate; He suffered and was buried; and the third day He rose again, according to the Scriptures; and ascended into heaven, and sitteth on the right hand of the Father; and He shall come again, with glory, to judge the quick and the dead; Whose kingdom shall have no end.

And I believe in the Holy Ghost, the Lord and Giver of Life; Who proceedeth from the Father and the Son; Who with the Father and the Son together is worshipped and glorified; Who spake by the prophets.

And I believe one holy catholic and apostolic Church. I acknowledge our baptism for the remission of sins; and I look for the resurrection of the dead, and the life of the world to come.

AMEN.

ATHANASIAN CREED

1. Whosoever will be saved, before all things it is necessary that he hold the catholic faith; 2. Which faith except every one do keep whole and undefiled, without doubt he shall perish everlastingly.

3. And the catholic faith is this: That we worship one God in Trinity, and Trinity in Unity; 4. Neither confounding the persons nor dividing the substance. 5. For there is one person of the Father, another of the Son, and another of the Holy Spirit. 6. But the Godhead of the Father, of the Son, and of the Holy Spirit is all one, the glory equal, the majesty co-eternal. 7. Such as the Father is, such is the Son, and such is the Holy Spirit. 8. The Father uncreate, the Son uncreate, and the Holy Spirit uncreate. 9. The Father incomprehensible, the Son incomprehensible, and the Holy Spirit incomprehensible. 10. The Father eternal, the Son eternal, and the Holy Spirit eternal. 11. And yet they are not three eternals but one eternal. 12. As also there are not three uncreated nor three incomprehensibles, but one uncreated and one incomprehensible. 13. So likewise the Father is almighty, the Son almighty, and the Holy Spirit almighty. 14. And yet they are not three almighties, but one almighty. 15. So the Father is God, the Son is God, and the Holy Spirit is God; 16. And yet they are not three Gods, but one God. 17. So likewise the Father is Lord, the Son Lord, and the Holy Spirit Lord; 18. And yet they are not three Lords but one Lord. 19. For like as we are compelled by the Christian verity to acknowledge every Person by himself to be God and Lord; 20. So are we forbidden by the catholic religion to say; There are three Gods or three Lords. 21. The Father is made of none, neither created nor begotten. 22. The Son is of the Father alone; not made nor created, but begotten. 23. The Holy Spirit is of the Father and of the Son; neither made, nor created, nor begotten, but proceeding. 24. So there is one Father, not three Fathers; one Son not three Sons; one Holy Spirit, not three Holy Spirits. 25. And in this Trinity none is afore or after another; none is greater or less than another. 26. But the whole three persons are co-eternal, and co-equal. 27. So that in all things, as aforesaid, the Unity in Trinity and the Trinity in Unity is to be worshipped. 28. He therefore that will be saved must thus think of the Trinity.

29. Furthermore it is necessary to everlasting salvation that he also believe rightly the incarnation of our Lord Jesus Christ. 30. For the right faith is that we believe and confess that our Lord Jesus Christ, the Son of God, is God and man. 31. God of the substance of the Father, begotten before the worlds; and man of substance of His mother, born in the world. 32. Perfect God and perfect man, of a reasonable soul and human flesh subsisting. 33. Equal to the Father as touching His Godhead, and inferior to the Father as touching His manhood. 34. Who, although He is God and man, yet He is not two, but one Christ. 35. One, not by conversion of the Godhead into flesh, but by taking of that manhood into God. 36. One altogether, not by confusion of substance, but by unity of person. 37. For as the reasonable soul and flesh is one man, so God and man is one Christ; 38. Who suffered for our salvation, descended into hell, rose again the third day from the dead; 39. He ascended into heaven, He sitteth on the right hand of the Father, God, Almighty; 40. From thence He shall come to judge the quick and the dead. 41. At whose coming all men shall rise again with their bodies; 42. and shall give account of their own works. 43. And they that have done good shall go into life everlasting, and they that have done evil into everlasting fire.

44. This is the catholic faith, which except a man believe faithfully, he cannot be saved.

THE FIVE POINTS OF CALVINISM

The **Five Points of Calvinism** are listed next to the star below. These points have some difficult words, but you will need to learn them. You can remember the order of these five points by looking at the first letter of each word. What word do these first letters spell?

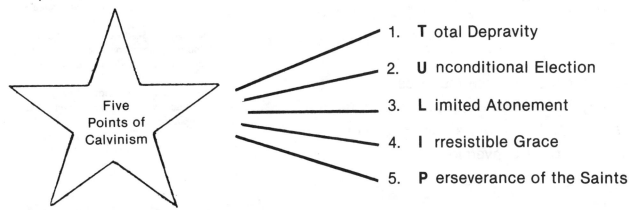

1. **T** otal Depravity
2. **U** nconditional Election
3. **L** imited Atonement
4. **I** rresistible Grace
5. **P** erseverance of the Saints

What do each of these five points mean?

TOTAL DEPRAVITY

"Total depravity" means that man is born sinful. Since our deep fall, we are born without any spiritual good.

God created us differently. God created us loving Him. Our hearts were created pointing in the following direction:

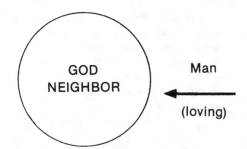

However, since our sinful fall in Paradise. we are now born totally depraved. Our hearts now point in the opposite direction:

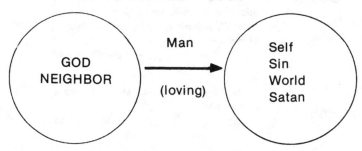

JOHN CALVIN

The Five Points of Calvinism are named after John Calvin. John Calvin was born in 1509. He became an important leader in the Protestant Reformation (the breaking away from many wrong doctrines and practices of the Roman Catholic Church, and the clear teaching of Scriptural truths in the church again.)

John Calvin wrote a book called **The Institutes of the Christian Religion**. This book became an important textbook of the Protestant Reformation. The truths of these five points are clearly explained in this book.

We cannot do any spiritual good as we are born. We are born loving ourselves, sin, the world, and Satan. In this condition, we are spiritually dead to loving and serving God. We are only alive to serving and loving ourselves and sin. Therefore, we need to be spiritually born again. We must be regenerated and converted by God. We need to be renewed and turned from loving sin to loving God.

And GOD saw that the **wickedness of man was great** in the earth, and that every imagination of the thoughts of his heart was only evil continually.
— Genesis 6:5

We cannot turn ourselves, because we are spiritually dead in sin. But God can turn us for He is almighty. Therefore, we must continually ask God for conversion.

The LORD looked down from heaven upon the children of men, to see if there were any that did understand, and seek God.
They are all gone aside, they are all together become filthy: *there is none that doeth good, no, not one.*
— Psalm 14:2-3

UNCONDITIONAL ELECTION

God created man perfectly sinless. But man chose to sin. Therefore, God could justly have left all people in their fallen condition. If God would have done this, then there would have been no hope of salvation for us, our parents, grandparents, or friends. There would be no need for a church or the Bible. There would be no possibility of salvation for sinful man. But what a wonder! God freely chose to save certain sinners. He chose to plant spiritual life in them and convert them.

To **elect** means to "choose." When God chose to save certain sinners, He chose these people **unconditionally.** This means that God did not chose these people because they were better than others. They also were totally depraved sinners. But God unconditionally elected to save them.

For He saith to Moses, *I will have mercy on whom I will have mercy,* and I will have compassion on whom I will have compassion.
So then it is not of him that willeth nor of him that runneth, but of God that sheweth mercy.
— Romans 9:15-16

God reveals His great love and mercy by electing to save some totally depraved sinners. God shows His great hatred for sin and His holy justice by punishing other sinners.

According as He hath **chosen us** in Him before the foundation of the world, that we should be holy and without blame before Him in love:
Having predestinated us unto the adoption of children by Jesus Christ to Himself, according to the good pleasure of His will.
— Ephesians 1:4-5

Salvation is entirely from God. It is a gift given freely by Him. Therefore, we must seek and ask Him for salvation.

Ye have not chosen Me, but *I have chosen you.*
— John 15:16a

LIMITED ATONEMENT

Atonement is the full payment for a wrong which has been done. Our fall in Paradise was a great wrongdoing. Now all people are sinners. Every time we sin, we sin against an almighty and eternal God. The price of sinning against an eternal God is eternal death!

The Lord Jesus, however, was willing to atone or pay for the sins of His elect people. He died for them as their substitute. He died to pay the full price for His guilty people. He died for them so that they could live eternally.

The number of the saved is **limited**. Jesus did not die as a substitute for all people. Not everyone is spoken free. Jesus only died as substitute for His elect children. They alone are spoken free.

I pray for them: I pray not for the world, but for them which Thou hast given Me; for they are Thine.
— John 17:9

He shall see of the travail of His soul, and shall be satisfied: by His knowledge shall My righteous servant justify **many;** for He shall bear their iniquities.
— Isaiah 53:11

For this is My blood of the new testament, which is shed for **many** for the remission of sins.
— Matthew 26:28

Husbands, love your wives, even as Christ also **loved the church,** and gave Himself for it.
— Ephesians 5:25

WHAT DO YOU THINK?

ATONEMENT FOR LITTLE JOE

Joe was playing softball with several other boys from his neighborhood in an empty lot.

It was Joe's turn to bat. He swung hard and hit an extra long foul ball. "Oh, no!" yelled several of the boys. Their yell was followed by a loud crash and the sound of breaking glass as the ball went right through a neighbor's front window.

The angry neighbor ran out of his house immediately. "Who did that?" he yelled. "Who hit that ball?"

"I did," answered Joe meekly.

"Well, then you will need to pay the full price," the man said. "That glass will cost $85 to replace!"

Poor Joe! He didn't have any money. What was he going to do? He tried to hold back his tears, but he could not. He just stood there and cried.

An older boy stepped forward. He felt sorry for Joe. "Mr. Morgan," he said to the man, "I will pay for the window." He ran home, returned, and paid the full price of $85. After paying, he turned to Joe. "Joe," he said, "you are free!"

This older boy **atoned** for Joe's wrong deed. What did Jesus do, in a much greater way, for all His people? Why is Jesus' atonement far greater than any atonement we can make for one another? Why is our guilt much greater?

IRRESISTIBLE GRACE

Grace is love and forgiveness shown to a person who does not deserve it. **Irresistible** means that which is so powerful that it cannot be stopped.

The Holy Spirit works saving grace in the hearts of all God's children in an irresistible, all-powerful way. Each person will resist God's saving grace because he is a totally depraved sinner. He wants to continue to serve himself, sin, and the world. This is what he wants. But the Holy Spirit will plant new spiritual life in a sinner's heart. He will turn the deepest desires of the person's heart to love and serve God. Then the person will be made willing to love and serve God.

And a certain woman named Lydia, a seller of purple, of the city of Thyatira, which worshipped God, heard us: whose heart the Lord opened, that *she attended unto the things which were spoken of Paul.*

— Acts 16:14

For it is God which worketh in you both *to will* and *to do* of His good pleasure.

— Philippians 2:13

For by *grace are ye saved* through faith; and that not of yourselves: it is the gift of God.

— Ephesians 2:8

Turn Thou us unto Thee, O LORD, and we *shall* be turned.

— Lamentations 5:21a

Thy people shall be *willing* in the day of Thy power.

— Psalm 110:3a

A person's heart is not renewed and turned by his own strength or desire. This is done by the power of the Holy Spirit working in his heart.

PERSEVERANCE OF THE SAINTS

To **persevere** means to continue and not fall away. **Saints** are God's true children. **Perseverance of the saints** means that God will keep all of His children in a regenerated and saved state. Those who are saved by God will remain saved forever. God will keep them in a saved condition.

Who are *kept* by the power of God through faith unto salvation ready to be revealed in the last time.

— I Peter 1:5

And I give unto them eternal life; and they shall *never perish,* neither shall any man pluck them out of My hand.

— John 10:28

Being confident of this very thing, that He which hath begun a good work in you *will perform it until the day of Jesus Christ.*

— Philippians 1:6

The Five Points of Calvinism teach five important doctrines of God's Word. All five show that salvation is entirely from God. All people are born as **totally depraved** sinners. However, God in His great mercy, has determined to **unconditionally elect** some sinners to salvation and eternal life. The Lord Jesus Christ died to **atone for the sins of His elect,** and the Holy Spirit will work saving **grace irresistibly** in their hearts. Finally, God will **preserve each of His saints** and bring them into everlasting life.

How wonderfully these truths exalt and praise God! What wonderful news these truths are for totally depraved and lost sinners! If God did not unconditionally elect, atone for, irresistibly work in, and preserve lost sinners, no person would ever be saved. True religion exalts God to the highest and brings man down to the lowest. Salvation is entirely from God.

God delights in graciously giving His wonderful salvation to sinners. Do you continually ask God to give and strengthen His grace in you? Do you also pray for this for others?

WHAT DO YOU THINK?

SEEK THE LORD

Imagine meeting a farmer who said, "I cannot make one seed grow; God, alone, can do that. God has decided in His plan whether my family and I will have food, shelter, and clothing in this coming year. Nothing I do, or do not do, will change this plan. Since everything depends upon God, I will sit back and do nothing."

If this man never went out to plant his field and had no harvest, who is at fault, God or this man? Why?

You will think that this man is acting very foolishly. Yet, there are people in church who reason in the same way. They think, "I cannot give myself spiritual life. I cannot convert myself. God alone can do that. God has also decided if I am elected or not. Nothing that I do, or do not do, will change that. Since everything depends upon God, I will sit back and do nothing."

These people never actively use the means of grace or prayerfully seek God. They never read the Bible or listen carefully when the Bible is read at church, school, and home. If these people are lost, who is at fault? Why? What must we do to be saved? What means of grace has God given us to prayerfully use?

MEMORIZATION WORK: Ephesians 1:3-6

CHAPTER CHECK-UP

1. What is a doctrinal standard? _____

   _____

   _____

2. Name our three doctrinal standards and the men who wrote each one:

Doctrinal Standard	**Author (s)**

   a. _____   _____

     _____

   b. _____   _____

     _____

   c. _____   _____

     _____

3. Name our three creeds:

   a. _____

   b. _____

   c. _____

4. Name the proper doctrinal standard to complete each of the following sentences:

   a. The _____ is divided into thirty-seven articles.

   b. The _____ is divided into fifty-two Lord's Days.

   c. The _____ is divided into five main heads of doctrine.

   d. The _____ explains the Five Points of Calvinism.

   e. The _____ is written with questions and answers.

5. How can you easily remember the order of the Five Points of Calvinism? _____

   _____

6. Write the name of each of the Five Points of Calvinism on the blank in front of its proper definition.

a. _____

                       Jesus Christ died to pay the full price for the sins of His elected people.

b. _____

                       God will uphold all of His children who are saved so that they will continue in their saved state.

c. _____

                       After the fall, man is born completely sinful and without spiritual good.

d. _____

                       The Holy Spirit will work all-powerfully in the heart of each of God's children to turn them from sin unto God.

e. _____

                       God freely chose to save certain lost sinners.

7. How do the Five Points of Calvinism:

a. Give all the honor for man's salvation to God?

_____

_____

b. Humble man to the lowest? _____

_____

_____

8. Why are the last four points of Calvinism the *only* hope of salvation for a totally depraved sinner?

_____

_____

_____

9. Since salvation is all of God, what must we do?

_____

_____

_____

CHAPTER FIFTEEN

REVIEW QUESTIONS

1. What is the difference between the "church" and a "church denomination"?

    _____

    _____

    _____

2. What is the:

    a. Church Visible? _____

    _____

    b. Church Invisible? _____

    _____

3. Name the two parts of the Church Invisible:

    a. _____   b. _____

4. Name the three offices in the church and the main duty of each office:

Office	*Main Duty*
a. _____	_____
_____	
b. _____	_____
_____	
c. _____	_____
_____	

5. How do the church offices today compare to the three anointed offices in the Old Testament?

    _____

    _____

    _____

CHAPTER SIXTEEN

REVIEW QUESTIONS

6. Name and describe each of our doctrinal standards and its author(s):

   a. Name:_____ Author(s):_____

      Description: _____

      _____

   b. Name:_____ Author(s):_____

      Description: _____

      _____

   c. Name:_____ Author(s):_____

      Description: _____

      _____

7. Which of our creeds:

   a. Is read most often in church?   _____

   b. Speaks clearly about the Trini-
      ty? (Three Persons in one God)   _____

   c. Speaks clearly about the two
      natures of Jesus Christ? (be-
      ing very God and very man)   _____

8. Name the Five Points of Calvinism:

   a. _____

   b. _____

   c. _____

   d. _____

   e. _____

9. The first letters of the above five points spell the word _____.

WORD SCRAMBLE

Unscramble each of the following NEW WORDS from Chapter 15 and 16 and write it on the blank below the scrambled letters. Then place the letter of the best matching meaning on the blank in front of the number.

Words

_____ 1. aetsr
_____

_____ 2. tetnsmtae
_____

_____ 3. rhhcuc
_____

_____ 4. tnyui
_____

_____ 5. nrhuhmcpurhtciat
_____

_____ 6. pratdviey
_____

_____ 7. tneuid
_____

_____ 8. lcoieetn
_____

_____ 9. mrsiipesno
_____

_____ 10. reevrpsneeac
_____

_____ 11. fceirroebafe
_____

_____ 12. rsesiiibertl
_____

_____ 13. hibsrulvceihc
_____

_____ 14. iocntudinonla
_____

_____ 15. natssi
_____

_____ 16. rhticcmlthiaun
_____

_____ 17. ercde
_____

_____ 18. nisrluibhecvhci
_____

_____ 19. tncaotdsrdirnalda
_____

_____ 20. nmtndianeoio
_____

Meanings

A. A man who holds a church office

B. An official statement of belief which often begins with the words, ''I believe''

C. Joined together

D. Agreement

E. The true believers in heaven who rejoice in God who conquered their enemies

F. All elected and converted children of God

G. A group of church people who meet under the same name and share the same doctrinal beliefs

H All-powerful; impossible to stop

I. All the people meeting together to worship God; the church which we can see

J. God's free choice to save certain sinners

K. The act of continuing

L. The Church Invisible fighting its sinful enemies on earth

M. An official explanation

N. Without any attached conditions; absolute

O. Weeds

P. The condition of being without any good and full of sin and evil; being spiritually dead in sin

Q. The believers in Christ from all over the world

R. All God's elect, the true believers who cannot be clearly seen by us

S. An official church statement and explanation of the Biblical truths believed

T. The effect from a certain idea or feeling

BIBLE STUDY QUESTIONS

Draw a line to connect each doctrinal truth with the text which most clearly teaches this truth.

Doctrinal Truths

1. Christ is the Head of His Church.

2. Not all members of the Church Visible are in the Church Invisible.

3. The Church Triumphant will be a large number of people from all over the world.

4. We are to respect our church office-bearers.

5. We are all born as totally depraved sinners.

6. Salvation is possible because God shows mercy to people and not because people first desire God.

7. Christ will keep each of His children in a state of grace; not one will be lost.

Texts

A.   Revelation 7:9

After this I beheld, and lo, a great multitude, which no man could number, of all nations, and kindreds, and people, and tongues, stood before the throne, and before the Lamb, clothed with white robes, and palms in their hands.

B.   I Timothy 5:17

Let the elders that rule well be counted worthy of double honour, especially they who labour in the word and doctrine.

C.   Romans 9:15-16

For He saith to Moses, I will have mercy on whom I will have mercy, and I will have compassion on whom I will have compassion.

So then it is not of him that willeth nor of him that runneth, but of God that sheweth mercy.

D.   Romans 2:28-29

For he is not a Jew, which is one outwardly; neither is that circumcision, which is outward in the flesh:

But he is a Jew, which is one inwardly; and circumcision is that of the heart, in the spirit, and not in the letter; whose praise is not of men, but of God.

E.   Ephesians 5:23

For the husband is the head of the wife, even as Christ is the head of the Church: and He is the Savior of the body.

F.   John 10:28

And I give unto them eternal life; and they shall never perish, neither shall any man pluck them out of My hand.

G.   Psalm 14:2-3

The LORD looked down from heaven upon the children of men, to see if there were any that did understand, and seek God.

They are all gone aside, they are all together become filthy: there is none that doeth good, no, not one.

THE MEANS OF GRACE
GOD'S WORD
GOD'S SACRAMENTS

NEW WORDS

1. Means of Grace — The Word of God and the sacraments

2. Instrument — A tool or that which is used to help perform a certain work

3. Mission — The bringing of the Word of God to people who have not heard it

4. Responsibility — A duty; a having to answer for one's behavior

5. Reject — To refuse; to cast away

6. Offer — To present something to be accepted or rejected

7. Sacraments — Signs and seals of God's grace; circumcision and the passover in the Old Testament, and baptism and the Lord's supper in the New Testament

8. Sign — A symbol; something we can see which speaks of a deeper meaning

9. Seal — Something which confirms and guarantees the truth

10. Official — Having proper authority; registered in the proper way

THE MEANS OF GRACE

The Holy Spirit uses two means of grace:

1. His Word; the Bible

2. His sacraments; baptism and the Lord's supper

The means of grace do not have power to work or strengthen faith of themselves. The Holy Spirit alone has this power. However, the Holy Spirit uses the means of grace as *instruments* or tools in His hands. He uses His Word and the sacraments to both work and strengthen faith in the hearts of His people.

And now, brethren, I commend you to God, and to the **Word of His grace,** which is able to build you up, and to give you an inheritance among all them which are sanctified.

— Acts 20:32

Go ye therefore, and **teach** all nations, **baptizing** them in the name of the Father, and of the Son, and of the Holy Ghost.

— Matthew 28:19

And when He had given thanks, He brake it, and said, Take, eat: this is My body, which is broken for you: this do in remembrance of Me.

After the same manner also He took the cup, when He had supped, saying, This cup is the new testament in My blood: this do ye, as oft as ye drink it, in remembrance of Me.

For as often as ye **eat this bread, and drink this cup,** ye do shew the Lord's death till He come.

— I Corinthians 11:24-26

WHO'S WORK IS IT?

Mr. Jason is a very skilled carpenter. He builds beautiful pieces of furniture. He uses different hand tools when building furniture.

One day a person came to see some of the beautiful furniture Mr. Jason had made. What would you think if he kept admiring Mr. Jason's hand tools? Who really built the furniture and should receive the credit? Mr. Jason's tools are important. But what is more important, the tools or the person using the tools?

What lesson can you learn from this story' when we speak of the Holy Spirit and the means of grace? Are the means of grace important? Why? However, what would the means of grace be without the Holy Spirit working through them?

How does Paul speak about this same truth in:

I Corinthians 3:5-7

Who then is Paul, and who is Apollos, but ministers by whom ye believed, even as the Lord gave to every man?

I have planted, Apollos watered; but God gave the increase.

So then neither is he that planteth any thing, neither he that watereth; but God that giveth the increase.

Only God the Holy Spirit can regenerate a person and strengthen his faith. The working of the Holy Spirit in our hearts is most necessary for all of us.

For as many as are led by the *Spirit of God,* they are the sons of God.
— Romans 8:14

Howbeit when He, the *Spirit of truth*, is come, He will guide you into all truth: for He shall not speak of Himself; but whatsoever He shall hear, that shall He speak: and He will shew you things to come.
— John 16:13

However, the means of grace are also very important. They are the means through which God has chosen to work.

So then faith cometh by hearing, and hearing **by the Word of God.**
— Romans 10:17

For whatsoever things were written aforetime were written for our learning, that we through patience and comfort of **the Scriptures** might have hope.
— Romans 15:4

GOD'S WORD

God will use **His Word,** the Bible, as a means to work and strengthen faith. God will bless the reading, teaching, and studying of His Word. He will especially bless the preaching of His Word.

How then shall they call on Him in whom they have not believed? and how shall they believe in Him of whom they have not heard? and how shall they hear without a preacher?

And how shall they preach, except they be sent? as it is written, How beautiful are the feet of them that **preach the gospel of peace**, and bring glad tidings of good things!
— Romans 10:14-15

For after that in the wisdom of God the world by wisdom knew not God, it pleased God by the foolishness of **preaching** to save them that believe.
— I Corinthians 1:21

God uses His Word to convert a person from loving sin to loving Him. He brings that person to His Word, or His Word to that person. How can you see this truth in the examples of the Ethiopian eunuch and the paralyzed man who was cured by Jesus? The Holy Spirit applies God's Word with power in the heart of this person. This renews his heart and turns him from sin to God. Sometimes this turning happens suddenly. At other times this takes place gradually over a longer period of time. Can you see the power of the Holy Spirit working through God's Word in the following stories?

WHAT DO YOU THINK?

. . . AND HE DIED

There once was an older man who strolled into a church. The minister read Genesis 5, a chapter which lists the generations from Adam to Noah. Each time the minister read about the end of a person's life, the man heard, . . . "and he died", . . . "and he died," . . . "and he died." These words were applied with power to his heart. They were the means which the Holy Spirit used to work his conversion to God.

Can you see the power of the Holy Spirit working through God's Word in this story?

— Adapted from *The Shorter Catechism Illustrated*

WHAT DO YOU THINK?

THE ETHIOPIAN EUNUCH

You can read the story of Philip and the Ethiopian eunuch in *Acts 8:26-39*. How did God care for the eunuch? Did God bring the preaching of His Word to the eunuch or the eunuch to the preaching of His Word?

THE PARALYZED MAN

You can read about the paralyzed man (the man sick of the palsy) in *Mark 2:1-12*. How did God care for this man? Did God bring His Word to this man or did He bring this man to His Word?

WHAT DO YOU THINK?

EVIL THOUGHTS BUT WONDERFUL RESULTS

George Whitefield was a famous minister who preached in both England and the United States. He was preaching outdoors to a large crowd at the city of Exeter. A man who hated his preaching brought a pocketful of stones to throw at Rev. Whitefield. He planned to hit him in the head.

As soon as the minister started preaching, the man took a stone out of his pocket. But the preaching of the Word of God seemed to go right through him. He soon dropped his stone!

This man later came to visit George Whitefield. He told him, "Sir, I came to hear you, planning to break your head; but the Spirit of God, through your preaching, broke my heart."

Can you see the power of the Holy Spirit working through God's Word here?

— Adapted from *The Shorter Catechism Illustrated*

Can you understand why we must read the Bible? Can you see why teaching and preaching from God's Word is so important? Do you listen very carefully at home, school, and church when the Bible is read, taught, and preached? Do you value your Bible? Do you prayerfully place yourself in God's way of means by reading, listening, and thinking about His Word? The Holy Spirit uses the Bible to work grace and spiritual growth in sinners' hearts. Can you see in the following stories how important it is to read the Bible and use the means of grace?

WHAT DO YOU THINK?

THE RICHEST JEWELS

A very rich lady was lying sick in bed for a long time. A God-fearing nurse had been taking care of her for several days. One day the sick woman said, "Go get my most expensive jewels." The nurse went and brought them to her. "Now, Nurse," said the lady, as she looked at each jewel, "wouldn't you like to have some of these jewels?"

"No, Ma'am," answered the nurse, "for I have jewels which are much richer than yours."

"How can that be?" asked the surprised lady. "Let me see one!"

"My jewels are in this Book," replied the nurse, taking her Bible from her purse. "I will show you some of them."

For several days the nurse showed her sick patient more and more of her jewels. God blessed His Word to the heart of this sick woman.

Why does the Bible contain the most precious jewels? Why are they far more valuable than the sick woman's jewels? Who is the "Pearl of Great Price" in the Bible?

WHAT DO YOU THINK?

THE FIRST WELSH BIBLES

Wales is one of the countries in the United Kingdom of Great Britain and Northern Ireland. In 1816, the people living in Wales received the Bible in their own language for the first time. When the first cart of Bibles arrived, the people filled the streets and flocked around it. Within a few minutes, every copy was gone. Soon people were seen sitting and reading their Bibles everywhere. Others crowded around and listened to those who read aloud.

Do you value your Bible? Do you love to read your Bible? How much time do you spend reading it every day? Do you value it more than any other gift?

— Adapted from *The Shorter Catechism Illustrated*

WHAT DO YOU THINK?

WHERE JESUS PASSES BY

"I wish that I had lived in Jericho at that time," said a young girl after hearing her mother read the story of Bartimaeus. "I wish that Jesus was passing by our city. If He was, I would run there to meet Him."

"You do not need to run that far," answered her mother. Pointing to her daughter's Bible which was lying beside her, she said, "Jesus is passing by much closer right now."

How is the answer of this mother true? What means does God use to work true saving faith and reveal Jesus Christ? Where must we place ourselves if we wish to be saved or grow in faith?

"Search the Scriptures; for in them ye think ye have eternal life: and they are they *which testify of Me."*

— John 5:39

WHAT DO YOU THINK?

THE MISSION COMMAND

We can read Christ's *"Mission* Command" to His apostles in Matthew 28:19-20:

Go ye therefore, and teach all nations, baptizing them in the name of the Father, and of the Son, and of the Holy Ghost:
Teaching them to observe all things whatsoever I have commanded you: and, lo, I am with you alway, even unto the end of the world. Amen.

Why is it so important to bring the means of grace to people who have never heard of the Word of God before? What did God promise would take place before the world would end?

And this gospel of the kingdom shall be preached in all the world for a witness unto all nations; and then shall the end come.

— Matthew 24:14

It is a great blessing to be brought up under the Word of God. It is a great privilege to have the Bible in our homes, schools, and churches. But it is also a great *responsibility!* God is speaking and offering His salvation to us in His Word.

By nature we are more interested in our own things than in God's offer. We love ourselves, sin, and the world. We do not want to love or follow God. Therefore, we must use His means. We must plead with God to bless His Word within us in a saving way. Otherwise our end will be terrible.

> Because *I have called, and ye refused;* I have stretched out My hand, and no man regarded;
> I also will laugh at your *calamity;* I will mock when your *fear* cometh.
> — Proverbs 1:24,26

WHAT DO YOU THINK?
A REJECTED INVITATION
Matthew 22:1-7:

And Jesus answered and spake unto them again by parables, and said,

The kingdom of heaven is like unto a certain king, which made a marriage for his son,

And sent forth his servants to call them that were bidden to the wedding: and they would not come.

Again, he sent forth other servants, saying, Tell them which are bidden, Behold, I have prepared my dinner: my oxen and fatlings are killed, and all things are ready: come unto the marriage.

But they made light of it, and went their ways, one to his farm, another to his merchandise:

And the remnant took his servants, and entreated them spitefully, and slew them.

But when the king heard thereof, he was wroth: and he sent forth his armies, and destroyed those murderers, and burned up their city.

What spiritual picture does this parable show us? What will happen to those who *reject* God's offer of salvation? How does this apply to people today? Why is this such a frightful and sad condition?

WHAT DO YOU THINK?

FOOLISHLY REFUSING A FREE GIFT!

A prince once traveled through a very poor area of a small city. He was shocked to see the old and ragged clothing of the people. When he returned to his palace, he sent a servant to visit these people. He commanded his servant, "*Offer* new clothing to everyone in trade for his old rags."

Expecting a great rush of people, the servant took other helpers with him. When they reached the poor area, he began to call, "New clothes — just trade in your old!" However, no one responded to his repeated callings.

The people did not believe him. Neither did they want to part with their old, ragged clothing. The servant could not understand why the people did not respond to his offer. "It's free!" he kept telling them. However, the more he tried to convince them, the more they turned away. Finally, he returned to his prince without anyone accepting his offer.

What do you think? Were these people foolish? Why? What does God offer to sinners in His Word and by His servants (true ministers)? Is this more valuable than the clothing offered by the prince in this story? How does man, by nature, respond to God's offer? What are some of the "rags" which natural man wants to keep rather than surrender to God? What beautiful clothing does he reject? If a person rejects God's offer of salvation, how is this so sad and costly?

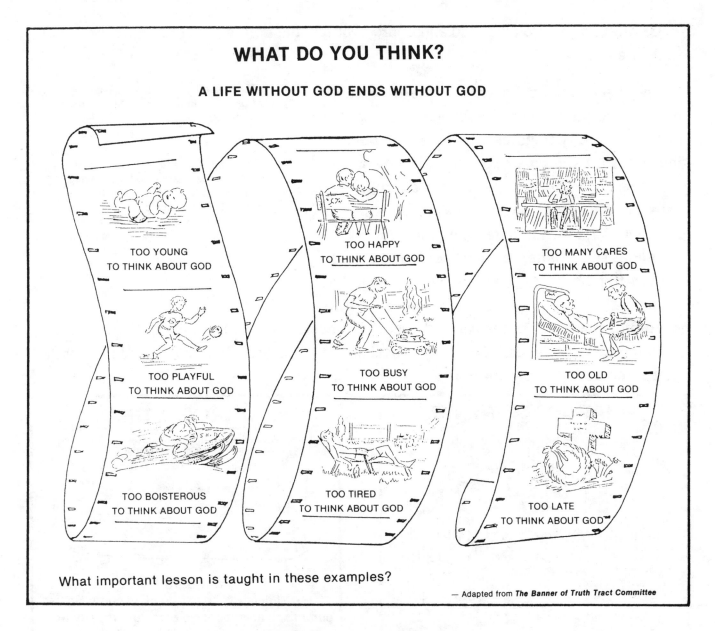

WHAT DO YOU THINK?

A LIFE WITHOUT GOD ENDS WITHOUT GOD

TOO YOUNG
TO THINK ABOUT GOD

TOO PLAYFUL
TO THINK ABOUT GOD

TOO BOISTEROUS
TO THINK ABOUT GOD

TOO HAPPY
TO THINK ABOUT GOD

TOO BUSY
TO THINK ABOUT GOD

TOO TIRED
TO THINK ABOUT GOD

TOO MANY CARES
TO THINK ABOUT GOD

TOO OLD
TO THINK ABOUT GOD

TOO LATE
TO THINK ABOUT GOD

What important lesson is taught in these examples?

— Adapted from *The Banner of Truth Tract Committee*

GOD'S SACRAMENTS

God has also given two New Testament **sacraments** as means of grace. The New Testament sacraments are:

1. Baptism
2. Lord's supper

Sacraments are based upon God's Word. They are means to strengthen faith in God's Word and promises. The Word of God is a means to both **work and strengthen** faith. The sacraments are a means to **strengthen** faith **only.**

A sacrament is a **sign** and **seal** of God's grace. A **sign** is something we can see. It speaks to us of a deeper meaning. A **seal** is an official stamp of approval. A seal proves something to be true. To what does the sign of water in baptism point?

Of what do the broken bread and poured wine at the Lord's supper remind us? What do they seal?

There are two sacraments in the New Testament church. The Lord Jesus gave these two sacraments to His church. They are **holy baptism** and the **Lord's supper.** God had also given two sacraments in the Old Testament church. They were **circumcision** and the **passover.** Both of these Old Testament sacraments included blood-shedding. This pointed to the shedding of Christ's blood. After Christ died, the full price for sin had been paid. His blood had been shed.

Go ye therefore, and teach all nations, **baptizing** them in the name of the Father, and of the Son, and of the Holy Ghost.
— Matthew 28:19

And He took **bread,** and gave thanks, and brake it, and gave unto them, saying, This is My body which is given for you: this do in remembrance of Me.
Likewise also the **cup** after supper, saying, This cup is the new testament in My blood, which is shed for you.
— Luke 22:19-20

Therefore, new forms of the two Old Testament sacraments were needed. Further blood shedding was not needed. Baptism now takes the place of circumcision, and the Lord's supper replaces the passover.

WHAT DO YOU THINK?

A SIGN

Angela had worked very hard on her math work all marking-period. When her report card was handed to her, she quickly looked. There was a "+" for effort and a "B" for her grade. She was very happy!

How are these two marks, the "+" and "B", both signs? What is the deeper meaning behind these marks? Why did Angela value these signs?

How are the broken bread and the poured wine at the Lord's supper signs? What is the deeper meaning behind these signs? Why are these signs valued so highly by God's true children?

WHAT DO YOU THINK?

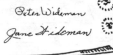

A SEAL

Mr. Wideman had to appear in court. He had purchased an expensive piece of property from another man and had paid him the full payment. Now the other man claimed that Mr. Wideman had never paid him all of the money.

Mr. Wideman had given the **official** paper for his purchase to his lawyer, but it seemed that this paper was lost. Mr. Wideman was very worried.

Suddenly, the lawyer came running into the court. "We found it! We found it!" he shouted. He showed Mr. Wideman the paper and then gave it to the judge. This was the official paper, sealed with the official seal of the city. The paper stated that the amount had been paid in full. The judge immediately spoke Mr. Wideman free!

Why did this sealed paper make such a difference? What is sealed to God's people in the sacraments? Why is this seal so important to them?

WHAT DO YOU THINK?

GOD'S RAINBOW

Noah, his sons, and their wives, lived through the "Great Flood" which covered the entire world. After the flood had ended and they left the ark, God promised that He would never destroy the whole earth with a flood again. God gave them a sign and a seal of His promise. We can read of this in:

Genesis 9:11-13

And I will **establish My covenant with you;** neither shall all flesh be cut off any more by the waters of a flood; neither shall there any more be a flood to destroy the earth.

And God said, This is the **token of the covenant** which I make between Me and you and every living creature that is with you, for perpetual generations:

I do set My **bow in the cloud,** and it shall be for a **token of a covenant** between Me and the earth.

After this, whenever the sky would become dark and it began to rain, Noah and his children might fear that another flood would come. How could they find comfort in seeing God's rainbow? Of which promise of God to His people are the sacraments a sign and seal? How can the sacraments be a means to strengthen their faith in God's promise?

The sacraments themselves do not strengthen faith. God the Holy Spirit uses the sacraments as a means to strengthen faith.

We need God for everything in our lives. We need Him to **work** spiritual life in us. We need Him to **strengthen** spiritual life after it has been planted in us. Are you seriously asking God to work in your heart and life? Are you prayerfully using God's means of grace each day?

MEMORIZATION QUESTIONS

1. What must the children do then?
   Pray, read God's Word, and be obedient.

2. What must children be mindful of?
   That I must at one time give an account of everything I do. II Corinthians 5:10

3. Where do we read this?
   In the sermon of Solomon.
   Ecclesiastes 11:9

4. What do we read there?
   But know thou, that for all these things God will bring thee into judgment.

5. What does the Lord say about those who seek Him early?
   That they shall find Him and obtain favor of the Lord.

6. And what does He say of those who hate Him?
   That they love death.

7. Where do we read this?
   Proverbs 8:35, 36

8. What do we read in verse 35?
   "For whoso findeth Me findeth life, and shall obtain favor of the Lord."

9. What do we read in verse 36?
   "But he that sinneth against Me wrongeth his own soul: all they that hate Me love death."

— Ledeboer's Catechism: Q. 71-79

CHAPTER CHECK-UP

1. Name the two means of grace which the Holy Spirit uses to strengthen faith:

   a. _____   b. _____

2. Who works through these means of grace and makes them powerful?

   _____

3. Why is it so important to place ourselves under the means of grace? _____

   _____

   _____

   _____

4. a. Why is mission work so important? _____

   _____

   b. Why should we strive to bring God's Word to all people? _____

   _____

   _____

5. If we have God's Word, how is this:

   a. A great blessing? _____

   _____

   _____

   b. A great responsibility? _____

   _____

   _____

6. Why will natural man, after his deep fall, not respond and agree with God's free offer of salvation?

   _____

   _____

CHAPTER CHECK-UP

7. Name the Old Testament and New Testament sacraments:

   Old Testament   **New Testament**

   a. _____   a. _____

   b. _____   b. _____

8. Why were new forms of the sacraments necessary in the New Testament?

   _____

   _____

9. A sacrament is a _____ and a _____
   of God's grace.

10. a. Who gave the Old Testament sacraments to the church?

    _____

    b. Who gave the New Testament sacraments to the church?

    _____

11. Who works through the sacraments to strengthen the faith of true believers?

    _____

12. Since we cannot save ourselves, what must we do?

    _____

    _____

13. What important lesson is taught in the "What Do You Think?" entitled,
    "A Life Without God Ends Without God" on page 91?_____

    _____

    _____

CHAPTER 18

HOLY BAPTISM

HOLY BAPTISM

Baptism is one of the two sacraments of the New Testament church. The Lord Jesus, as King of His church, commanded His church to be baptized.

> Go ye therefore, and teach all nations, **baptizing** them in the name of the Father, and of the Son, and of the Holy Ghost.
> — Matthew 28:19

We use water to wash ourselves. Being baptized with water pictures the washing away of sin through the blood of Jesus Christ. All people are born in sin and live sinful lives. This makes everyone unclean in God's sight. We all need to be washed clean from our sins. The only way this is possible is through Christ's death for us. We all need the truth which baptism pictures unto us.

> And now why tarriest thou? arise, and be **baptized,** and wash away thy sins, calling on the name of the Lord.
> — Acts 22:16

> Then Peter said unto them, Repent, and be **baptized** everyone of you in the name of Jesus Christ for the remission of sins, and ye shall receive the gift of the Holy Ghost.
> — Acts 2:38

If Christ washes us from our sins, we become one of His children. Then we are

97

THE BAPTISM OF THE EUNUCH

We can read about the baptism of the Ethiopian eunuch in:

Acts 8:36-39:

> And as they went on their way, they came unto a certain water: and the eunuch said, See, here is water; what doth hinder me to be baptized?
>
> And Philip said, If thou believest with all thine heart, thou mayest. And he answered and said, I believe that Jesus Christ is the Son of God.
>
> And he commanded the chariot to stand still: and they went down both into the water, both Philip and the eunuch; and he baptized him.
>
> And when they were come up out of the water, the Spirit of the Lord caught away Philip, that the eunuch saw him no more: and he went on his way rejoicing.

How can you see from this story that the water used in baptism is ordinary and not special water?

spiritually born again as children of God. We then become true members of His church. Baptism speaks of this. Baptism points to the washing away of sin, being born again spiritually, and becoming a member of Christ's church. All this is possible through the death of Jesus Christ.

> For by one Spirit are we all **baptized** into one body, whether we be Jews or Gentiles, whether we be bond or free; and have been all made to drink into one Spirit.
> — I Corinthians 12:13

Ordinary water is used in baptism. It is not "special" water or "holy" water. We wash ourselves with ordinary water to become clean. Ordinary water is also used in baptism to picture spiritual washing from the filthiness of sin.

> Can any man forbid **water,** that these should not be baptized, which have received the Holy Ghost as well as we?
> And he commanded them to be baptized in the name of the Lord. Then prayed they him to tarry certain days.
> — Acts 10:47-48

Baptism must be done:

1. In the Name of God the Father, God the Son, and God the Holy Ghost.

2. By an ordained minister

> Go **ye** therefore, and teach all nations, baptizing them **in the name of the Father, and of the Son, and of the Holy Ghost.**
> — Matthew 28:19

Baptism is very important. The Lord Jesus commanded that His church should be baptized. It is one of the means of grace which God has given to strengthen faith.

> He that believeth and is *baptized,* shall be *saved;* but he that believeth not shall be damned.
>
> — Mark 16:16

However, baptism does not actually wash away our sins. It does not actually give faith. It points to these things. A person who is *not* baptized *can* be saved. Also, a person who *is* baptized *can* be lost. Our baptism is a great blessing. But we need the power of the Holy Spirit to work through our baptism for it to be saving. The Holy Spirit must apply the true meaning of baptism to our hearts.

> For in Jesus Christ *neither circumcision availeth any thing, nor uncircumcision;* but faith which worketh by love.
>
> — Galatians 5:6

WHAT DO YOU THINK?

The Thief on the Cross

AN UNBAPTIZED PERSON SAVED

You can read of the true conversion of the thief on the cross in:

Luke 23:39-43:

And one of the malefactors which were hanged railed on him, saying, If Thou be the Christ, save Thyself and us.

But the other answering rebuked him, saying, Dost not thou fear God, seeing thou art in the same condemnation?

And we indeed justly; for we receive the due reward of our deeds: but this Man hath done nothing amiss.

And he said unto Jesus, Lord, remember me when Thou comest into Thy kingdom.

And Jesus said unto him, Verily I say unto thee, Today shalt thou be with Me in paradise.

This man was saved and taken into heaven by Jesus. Do we read in the Bible that he was a Christian before or that he was baptized?

Can an unbaptized person be saved?

WHAT DO YOU THINK?

Simon the Sorcerer

A BAPTIZED PERSON LOST

We can read about Simon the Sorcerer in:

Acts 8:13, 18-23:

Then Simon himself believed also: and when he was baptized, he continued with Philip, and wondered, beholding the miracles and signs which were done.

And when Simon saw that through laying on of the apostles' hands the Holy Ghost was given, he offered them money,

Saying, Give me also this power, that on whomsoever I lay hands, he may receive the Holy Ghost.

But Peter said unto him, Thy money perish with thee, because thou hast thought that the gift of God may be purchased with money.

Thou hast neither part nor lot in this matter: for thy heart is not right in the sight of God.

Repent therefore of this thy wickedness, and pray God, if perhaps the thought of thine heart may be forgiven thee.

For I perceive that thou art in the gall of bitterness, and in the bond of iniquity.

Can a baptized person go lost?

Baptism has been performed in three different ways by the New Testament church. These three ways are:

1. *Sprinkling* — Sprinkling water on a person, usually on the forehead.

2. *Pouring* — Pouring water over a person.

3. *Immersing* — Putting a person entirely under the water.

The Bible does not tell us whether **sprinkling, pouring,** or **immersing** was used when the apostles baptized. Each of these three ways pictures the same truth. Each is a sign of a sinner being washed clean by the blood of Jesus Christ. Therefore, all three ways of baptizing may be used by the church.

God's Word teaches us that baptism is only for believing adults and their children.

> And He said unto them, Go ye into all the world, and preach the gospel to every creature.
> **He that believeth and is baptized shall be saved;** but he that believeth not shall be damned.
> — Mark 16:15-16

God's "mission command" to His church is recorded in Mark 16:15-16. When a missionary minister goes into a new country, the people there have not heard of God's Word. Therefore, he may not baptize these people. He must follow this order:

1. He must first preach.
2. Adults must believe and confess their belief.
3. Only then may they be baptized with their children.

Children are included in a church and Covenant of Grace relationship. They are placed under God's Word and are outwardly separated from the world. Therefore, God commanded children in the Old Testament to be circumcised and children in the New Testament to be baptized.

WHAT DO YOU THINK?

Abraham

ARE CHILDREN OF BELIEVERS INCLUDED?

Read Genesis 17:9-10, 12, 26-27. Who were commanded by God to receive the mark of circumcision?

And God said unto Abraham, Thou shalt keep My covenant therefore, thou, and thy seed after thee in their generations.

This is My covenant, which ye shall keep, between Me and you and thy seed after thee; Every man child among you shall be circumcised.

And he that is eight days old shall be circumcised among you, every man child in your generation, he that is born in the house, or bought with money of any stranger, which is not of thy seed.

In the selfsame day was Abraham circumcised, and Ishmael his son.

And all the men of his house, born in the house, and bought with money of the stranger, were circumcised with him.

Baptism replaced circumcision. Who are to receive the mark of baptism?

Acts 16:14-15

And a certain woman named Lydia, a seller of purple, of the city of Thyatira, which worshipped God, heard us: whose heart the Lord opened, that she attended unto the things which were spoken of Paul.

And when she was baptized, and her household, she besought us, saying, If ye have judged me to be faithful to the Lord, come into my house, and abide there. And she constrained us.

Acts 2:39

For the promise is unto you, and to your children, and to all that are afar off, even as many as the Lord our God shall call.

Mark 10:13-14

And they brought young children to Him, that He should touch them: and His disciples rebuked those that brought them.

But when Jesus saw it, He was much displeased, and said unto them, Suffer the little children to come unto Me, and forbid them not: for of such is the kingdom of God.

WHAT DO YOU THINK?

THE BAPTISM OF BELIEVING ADULTS AND THEIR CHILDREN

Paul was a missionary minister in the New Testament time. What type of adults did Paul baptize? What was necessary in order to be baptized into the church as an adult? After a believing adult was baptized, who could then also be baptized? Answer these questions from the following examples.

Lydia

And a certain woman named Lydia, a seller of purple, of the city of Thyatira, which worshipped God, heard us: whose heart the Lord opened, that she attended unto the things which were spoken of Paul.

And when **she was baptized, and her household,** she besought us, saying, If ye have judged me to be faithful to the Lord, come into my house, and abide there. And she constrained us.

— Acts 16:14-15

Philippian Jailer

And they spake unto him the word of the Lord, and to all that were in his house.

And he took them the same hour of the night, and washed their stripes; and was baptized, **he and all his,** straightway.

— Acts 16:32-33

Our baptism is a great blessing. This blessing is not given to everyone. Millions of children in the world are not baptized.

My baptism gives me the following outward blessings or privileges:

1. It confirms me as a member of God's church (the Church Visible).
2. It places me under God's Word. God has promised to bless His Word to save sinners. The Holy Spirit will apply God's Word to the hearts of many. It places me under the callings and invitations of the gospel.
3. It includes me continually in the prayers of the church.
4. It places God's mark upon me. Baptism separates me from the world and places me in an outward relationship to God's Covenant of Grace.

I may **plead** in prayer to God and say, "Lord, please remember me in Thy mercy. I am baptized in Thy Name. Thou hast placed Thy mark on my forehead. Please, Lord, bless Thy Word and all the outward benefits of my baptism in a saving way to me. Please give me the deepest truth of which my baptism is a sign. Wash me clean from all my sins!"

Baptism is such a great blessing. It places us near the way of salvation. It places us under the means of grace which God has promised to bless to work salvation in the hearts of His elect children.

These great benefits of baptism make us more responsible before God. God will ask each of us what we have done with all the blessings He has given to us. The more blessings the Lord gives, the more He will require from us.

> And that servant, which knew his lord's will, and prepared not himself, neither did according to his will, shall be beaten with many stripes.
>
> But he that knew not, and did commit things worthy of stripes, shall be beaten with few stripes. For **unto whomsoever much is given, of him shall be much required:** and to whom men have committed much, of him they will ask the more.
> — Luke 12:47-48

WHAT DO YOU THINK?

BAPTIZED OR UNBAPTIZED?

Moravian missionaries had been working for some time in a village in Greenland. A certain man, who was respected by the people, lived in this village. He had firmly decided to stay in his old ways. He would not attend church or be baptized.

However, his daughter became converted and was baptized. Her father angrily asked her what she had done. She calmly answered him by telling him of the happiness she had found. She ended her answer by saying, "Father, you can also be this happy. But if you will not, I cannot stay and perish with you!"

These words broke the heart of this proud father. He began to attend church with his daughter.

Did this daughter value baptism? Was the fear of God or the fear of man stronger in her life?

— Adapted from *The Shorter Catechism Illustrated*

We are baptized and live under God's Word. We are members of church. If we still go lost, our judgment will be far more severe than the judgment of those who have never heard of God's Word and were never baptized.

God has placed His mark upon us and separated us from the world. He has placed us in His Church Visible and under His Word. This mark of separation should be seen in

WHAT DO YOU THINK?

BRANDED WITH THE MARK OF ITS OWNER

When a young calf is born on a ranch, the ranch hands must brand the new calf. They mark it as one of their own.

How can baptism be compared with this example? If we are baptized, whose mark do we bear? To whom do we belong? How does God refer to His "marked" people in:

Deuteronomy 7:6:

For thou art an holy people unto the LORD thy God: the LORD thy God hath chosen thee to be a special people unto Himself, above all people that are upon the face of the earth.

If all church members are separated and marked by God, does this mean that all are truly saved? Why not?

our lives. Our thoughts, words, and actions should be different from the rest of the world. We should live according to God's Word. Can this difference be seen in your life? Are you carefully trying to watch what you say and do?

Ye shall observe to do therefore as the LORD your God hath commanded you: ye shall not turn aside to the right hand or to the left.

Ye shall walk in all the ways which the LORD your God hath commanded you, that ye may live, and that it may be well with you, and that ye may prolong your days in the land which ye shall possess.

— Deuteronomy 5:32-33

And now, Israel, what doth the LORD thy God require of thee, but to fear the LORD thy God, to walk in all His ways, and to love Him, and to serve the Lord thy God with all thy heart and with all thy soul,

To keep the commandments of the LORD, and His statutes, which I command thee this day for thy good?

— Deuteronomy 10:12-13

Our baptism is a great blessing and a great responsibility. But it is not enough to save us. We need the actual washing away of our sins by the Lord Jesus Christ in our lives. This is the deepest truth of baptism.

WHAT DO YOU THINK?

AFRAID TO BE DIFFERENT

Bob went to a friend's birthday party. Several other boys were there too. Bob was the only boy at this party who was baptized and attended church.

One of the boys often used bad words to sound "big" or "tough." Soon all the other boys did as well. Poor Bob! He did not want to be different or have the others think he was a "sissy." So he also spoke some of the same bad words. His conscience warned him, but he did it anyway.

Bob is responsible to God for his baptism. Could his mark of baptism be seen here? Was he showing that he was separated and marked by God? Can your friends tell from your words and actions that you are baptized?

Our baptism places us in an outward relationship to the Covenant of Grace. It separates us outwardly from the world. Can you see why we are so responsible for the blessings which we receive from baptism?

When do the sign and seal of baptism become true for us in the deepest sense? This only becomes true for us when the Holy Spirit powerfully applies the truth of baptism in our hearts. Only then are we actually turned from loving self to loving God. Only then do we become true children of God in an inward and eternal covenant relationship. The following texts and chart can help you see this more clearly.

BAPTIZED AND UNCONVERTED — AN OUTWARD RELATIONSHIP

An Outward and Breakable Relationship to the Covenant of Grace

Not according to the covenant that I made with their fathers in the day that I took them by the hand to bring them out of the land of Egypt; which **My covenant they brake,** although I was an husband unto them, saith the LORD.

— Jeremiah 31:32

But the **children of the kingdom shall be cast out** into outer darkness: there shall be weeping and gnashing of teeth.

— Matthew 8:12

I know that ye are **Abraham's seed;** but ye seek to kill Me, because **My word hath no place in you.**

They answered and said unto Him, Abraham is our father. Jesus saith unto them, If ye were Abraham's children, ye would do the works of Abraham. — John 8:37, 39

That is, They which are the children of the flesh, **these are not the children of God:** but the children of the promise are counted for the seed.

As it is written, **Jacob have I loved, but Esau have I hated.**

— Romans 9:8, 13

Outward, but not Inward Church Members

For he is not a Jew, which is one outwardly; neither is that circumcision, which is outward in the flesh:

But he is a Jew, which is one **inwardly;** and circumcision is that of the heart, in the spirit, and not in the letter: whose praise is not of men, but of God.

— Romans 2:28-29

For they are not all Israel, which are of Israel:

Neither, because they are the seed of Abraham, are they all children: but in Isaac shall thy seed be called.

— Romans 9:6b-7a

BAPTIZED AND CONVERTED — AN INWARD RELATIONSHIP

An Inward and Unbreakable Relationship to the Covenant of Grace

For the mountains shall depart, and the hills be removed; but My kindness shall not depart from thee, **neither shall the covenant of My peace be removed,** saith the LORD that hath mercy on thee.

— Isaiah 54:10

Nevertheless My lovingkindness will I not utterly take from him, nor suffer My faithfulness to fail.

My covenant will I not break, nor alter the thing that is gone out of My lips.

— Psalm 89:33-34

For as many as are **led by the Spirit of God,** they are the **Sons of God.** — Romans 8:14

That ye may be blameless and harmless, **the sons of God,** without rebuke, in the midst of a crooked and perverse nation, among whom ye **shine as lights in the world.**

— Philippians 2:15

For this is the covenant that I will make with the house of Israel after those days, saith the Lord; I will put My laws into their mind, and write them in their hearts: and **I will be to them a God, and they shall be to Me a people.** Hebrews 8:10

Inward, Living, Spiritual Church Members

Jesus answered and said unto him, Verily, verily, I say unto thee, Except a man be **born again,** he cannot see the kingdom of God.

— John 3:3

My sheep hear My voice, and **I know them, and they follow Me:**

And I give unto them eternal life; and they shall never perish, neither shall any man pluck them out of My hand.

My Father, which gave them Me, is greater than all; and no man is able to pluck them out of My Father's hand.

— John 10:27-29

COVENANT OF GRACE

JESUS CHRIST

— Head of the Covenant of Grace
— Head of the Church

THE WORLD
THE CHURCH
THE CHURCH OUTWARDLY
THE CHURCH INWARDLY

NON-SAVING
SAVING
THE BAPTIZED
THE UNBAPTIZED

BY SPIRITUAL REBIRTH: BY BEING BORN AGAIN

BY NATURAL BIRTH: BY BAPTISM

INWARD

a. Covenant Relationship
b. Church Membership
c. Children of God

By Regeneration

OUTWARD

a. Covenant Relationship
b. Church Membership

By Baptism

INWARD COVENANT RELATIONSHIP (Baptism applied *Inwardly*)	OUTWARD COVENANT RELATIONSHIP (Baptism applied *Outwardly*)
An *inward* relationship to the Covenant of Grace includes:	An *outward* relationship to the Covenant of Grace by baptism includes:
Inward and eternal spiritual blessings	*Outward* blessings of separation from the world
An *unbreakable* relationship to God's Covenant of Grace	A *breakable* relationship to God's Covenant of Grace
Coming under God's *inward call:* the regenerating and converting work of the Holy Spirit	Coming under God's *outward call:* His Word, the invitation of the gospel, and the teachings, prayers, and warnings of the church, which God often blesses to work salvation.
These are the *greatest* blessings: true conversion and salvation	These are *great* blessings, but not enough to be saved.

WHAT DO YOU THINK?

NICODEMUS

Nicodemus was a child of Abraham. He was a circumcised Jew. He was a member of, and a chief ruler in, the church.

Yet when Jesus spoke to him, He said:

> Verily, verily, I say unto thee, Except a man be born again, he cannot see the kingdom of God.
> Nicodemus saith unto Him, How can a man be born when he is old? can he enter the second time into his mother's womb, and be born?
> Jesus answered, Verily, verily, I say unto thee, Except a man be born of water and of the Spirit, he cannot enter into the kingdom of God.
> That which is born of the flesh is flesh; and that which is born of the Spirit is spirit.
> Marvel not that I said unto thee, Ye must be born again.
> The wind bloweth where it listeth, and thou hearest the sound thereof, but canst not tell whence it cometh, and whither it goeth: so is every one that is born of the Spirit.
> — John 3:3b-8

Was Nicodemus related to the Covenant of Grace in an outward or inward way? Was he an outward or an inward child of God? What did Jesus teach was necessary in order to become a child of God inwardly?

We all need God to make the deepest meaning of baptism true in our lives. We need to be born spiritually. This must be worked by the Holy Spirit. We are then brought into a wonderful, eternal, and saving relationship with God.

Our baptism places us under God's means of grace. God has promised to bless His Word to the salvation of many people. God is almighty. He delights in saving sinners. Do you pray and plead with God to bless the means of grace to you in a saving way?

> And I say unto you, **Ask,** and it shall be given you; **seek,** and ye shall find; **knock,** and it shall be opened unto you.
> — Luke 11:9

> If My people, which are called by My name, shall **humble themselves,** and **pray,** and **seek My face,** and **turn from their wicked ways;** then will I hear from heaven, and will forgive their sin, and will heal their land.
> — II Chronicles 7:14

> I love them that love Me; and those that **seek** Me early shall find Me.
> — Proverbs 8:17

WHAT DO YOU THINK?

SEEING PAUL'S MARK OF BAPTISM

Paul was walking home with several other boys who lived in his neighborhood. They had been playing football on the school playground.

As they were walking and talking, one of the older boys named Tom said, "Hey! I know what we should do!"

"What?" asked the others.

"Up ahead," Tom continued, "is old lady Smithers' house. You know how she yelled at us for running across her lawn, right? Well, I have a perfect plan!"

The other boys listened as Tom told his plan. "We'll wait for about twenty minutes, and then it will be dark. You know she has a lot of tomato plants in her back garden, right? We can sneak across her fence and each grab three or four tomatoes. Then we'll come back around to the front of her house and plaster the front of her house with all the tomatoes at the same time!"

The other boys laughed and jumped up and down at the thought. They were excited about Tom's plan. Paul, however, did not laugh or say anything. Paul was baptized and attended a church and Christian school. His conscience spoke up immediately. He knew this plan was clearly wrong and mean.

Tom noticed that Paul was not laughing like the others. "What's the matter, Paul?" he asked, "Are you scared?" The other boys all laughed again.

"No," Paul answered, "I'm not scared, but I'm not going to do that. Mrs. Smithers' worked hard to grow her tomatoes, and who will clean up the mess for her? It is just plain mean to do that."

As he turned away and started walking home, the other boys kept laughing and calling out behind him, "Good-bye, **good** boy!" "Don't do anything **mean** now!" "Behave **nicely** for Mommy!" Paul tried to ignore all the comments and laughter, but he felt the sting of these remarks.

When he entered his bedroom, he opened his Bible to read a chapter. He opened it to Matthew 5 and started reading. He soon came to verses 11 and 12:

Blessed are ye, when men shall revile you, and persecute you, and shall say all manner of evil against you falsely, for My sake.

Rejoice, and be exceeding glad: for great is your reward in heaven: for so persecuted they the prophets which were before you.

These verses comforted him. He knew he had done the right thing. God would make all things well.

Paul is responsible to God for his baptism. Could his mark of baptism be seen clearly in this story? Can your mark of baptism be seen clearly by your friends?

WHAT DO YOU THINK?

BRINGING FORTH FRUIT

We can read the Parable of the Barren Fig Tree in:

Luke 13:6-9

He spake also this parable; A certain man had a fig tree planted in his vineyard; and he came and sought fruit thereon, and found none.

Then said he unto the dresser of his vineyard, Behold, these three years I come seeking fruit on this fig tree, and find none: cut it down; why cumbereth it the ground?

And he answering said unto him, Lord, let it alone this year also, till I shall dig about it, and dung it:

And if it bear fruit, well: and if not, then after that thou shalt cut it down.

A vineyard is often used in the Bible as a picture of God's church. Who is the owner of the vineyard? Who is the fig tree that does not bring forth any fruit? What is the fruit? How can we see the owner's patience? If in the end the tree still does not bring forth fruit, what will happen to it?

How is this a warning to all outward church-goers who are baptized, but do not bring forth true fruits of love unto God and their neighbors? What will happen to such baptized members of the church?

MEMORIZATION QUESTIONS

1. Must we pray to Him for His Spirit?
   Yes, certainly. Matthew 7:7

2. Have we a warrant thereto?
   Yes, in our baptism.

3. In whose name are you baptized?
   In the name of the Father and of the Son and of the Holy Ghost. Matthew 28:19

4. Is it enough that you are baptized?
   No, I must be cleansed from my sins in the blood of the Lord Jesus. I John 1:7

5. How is faith strengthened?
   By the use of the sacraments.

6. What is a sacrament?
   A sign and seal of God's grace.
   Romans 4:11

7. How many sacraments do we have?
   Two: Holy Baptism and the Holy Supper.
   I Corinthians 12:13

8. What does Baptism signify?
   The washing away of sins. Acts 22:16

9. Can water wash away sins?
   No; Christ's blood cleanses us from all sin. I John 1:7

10. Why ought we to baptize children?
    Because they are in the Covenant of God.
    Acts 2:39

— Ledeboer's Catechism, Q. 42-45
— Borstius' Catechism: Lesson XXIV, Q. 1-6

CHAPTER CHECK-UP

1. a. Baptism is a sign or picture of: _____
    _____

    b. Baptism makes us a member of: _____
    _____

2. The water used in baptism is _____ water.

3. To be a true baptism, the following two things are necessary:

    a. _____
    _____

    b. _____
    _____

4. Answer "yes" or "no":

    a. Does baptism actually wash away a person's sin? _____

    b. Can a person be saved without being baptized? _____ Name an
    example in the Bible: _____

    c. Can a person who is baptized go lost? _____ Name an example
    in the Bible: _____

5. In what three ways has the church performed baptism? Explain what each one
    means:

    a. _____ — _____
    _____

    b. _____ — _____
    _____

    c. _____ — _____
    _____

CHAPTER CHECK-UP

6. a. When a missionary minister begins working in a new mission field, which adults may be baptized? _____

   _____

   _____

   b. Give two examples of this from the Bible:

      1. _____

      2. _____

7. Name four outward blessings or privileges which we receive when we are baptized:

   a. _____

   b. _____

   c. _____

   d. _____

8. Why am I, because of my baptism, more responsible to God than a person who was never baptized? _____

   _____

   _____

9. Why is my outward baptism not enough for salvation? What do I need to be saved? _____

   _____

   _____

10. How should our marks of baptism be seen by others?

   _____

   _____

REVIEW QUESTIONS

1. Why is it so important to place ourselves under the preaching and reading of the Word of God? _____

    _____

2. God will use His Word to both _____ and _____ faith.

3. Give an example from the Bible of:

    a. The Word of God being brought to a person — _____

    _____

    b. A person being brought to the Word of God — _____

    _____

4. Who uses the Bible as a means when powerfully converting? _____

5. Why does natural man reject God's offer of grace?

    _____

    _____

6. How are the sacraments:

    a. A sign? — _____

    _____

    b. A seal? — _____

    _____

7. Why were new forms of the two Old Testament sacraments necessary after Christ died? _____

    _____

    _____

REVIEW QUESTIONS

8. Why is "water" used as a sign in baptism? _____

    _____

9. What two requirements are necessary for a baptism to be considered official

    by the church?

    a. _____

    b. _____

10. Name the order a missionary minister must follow when baptizing in a new

    mission area:

    a. _____

    b. _____

    c. _____

11. How is our baptism a great:

    a. Blessing? _____

    _____

    _____

    b. Responsibility? _____

    _____

    _____

12. Outward baptism separates us from the _____ and places us in the

    _____ Visible. It places me under the _____ of God

    and in an _____ relationship to the Covenant of _____.

13. Why do we need more than outward baptism to be saved? _____

14. How should your mark of baptism be seen in your life?

    _____

    _____

CODED WORDS

Can you solve this code and find all of the NEW WORDS from Chapters 17 and 18? Each number stands for one letter. Write the correct NEW WORD on the blank below the coded word. Then place the letter of the best meaning on the blank in front of the matching number.

_____ 1. 8-26-24-9-26-14-22-13-7-8

_____ 2. 14-18-8-8-18-12-13

_____ 3. 26-11-11-15-2

_____ 4. 8-18-20-13

_____ 5. 11-12-6-9-18-13-20

_____ 6. 11-9-18-5-18-15-22-20-22

_____ 7. 14-22-26-13-8-12-21-20-9-26-24-22

_____ 8. 8-22-5-22-9-22

_____ 9. 12-21-21-22-9

_____ 10. 21-18-15-7-19-18-13-22-8-8

_____ 11. 9-22-17-22-24-7

_____ 12. 18-13-5-18-7-26-7-18-12-13

_____ 13. 18-13-8-7-9-6-14-22-13-7

_____ 14. 12-9-23-18-13-26-9-2

_____ 15. 12-21-21-18-24-18-26-15

_____ 16. 11-15-22-26-23

_____ 17. 9-22-8-11-12-13-8-18-25-18-15-18-7-2

_____ 18. 18-14-14-22-9-8-18-12-13

_____ 19. 8-22-26-15

_____ 20. 8-11-9-18-13-16-15-18-13-20

A. A favor or blessing given to some people instead of others

B. Baptizing by applying drops of water to a person

C. A tool or that which is used to perform a certain work

D. A symbol; something we see which speaks of a deeper meaning

E. Dirtiness; being full of sin

F. Usual or normal

G. The bringing of the Word of God to people who have not heard it

H. Baptizing by pouring water over a person

I. To refuse; to cast away

J. A request which asks a person to attend

K. Having proper authority; properly registered

L. To attach; to put or place upon

M. A duty; a having to answer for

N. To pray; to ask

O. The Bible and the sacraments

P. Holy baptism and the Lord's supper

Q. Baptizing by putting a person entirely under the water

R. Something which confirms and guarantees the truth

S. Very strict, serious, or deep

T. To present something to be accepted or rejected

BIBLE STUDY QUESTIONS

Draw a line to connect each doctrinal truth with the text which most clearly teaches this truth.

Doctrinal Truths

1. We need God the Holy Spirit to teach us spiritual truths.

2. God the Holy Spirit teaches through the means of His Word.

3. It is a serious sin to refuse God's call and invitation to salvation.

4. Jesus Christ has commanded His church to baptize its members.

5. Baptism is a sign and seal of the washing away of sin through Jesus Christ.

6. People who are in an outward relationship to Christ's church and kingdom can fall away and be cast out forever.

7. To be in an inward and saving relationship with Christ, we first need to be spiritually born again.

Texts

A.   Proverbs 1:24, 26

Because I have called, and ye refused; I have stretched out My hand, and no man regarded;

I also will laugh at your calamity; I will mock when your fear cometh.

B.   Acts 2:38

Then Peter said unto them, Repent, and be baptized every one of you in the name of Jesus Christ for the remission of sins, and ye shall receive the gift of the Holy Ghost.

C.   John 16:13

Howbeit when He, the Spirit of truth, is come, He will guide you into all truth: for He shall not speak of Himself; but whatsoever He shall hear, that shall He speak: and He will shew you things to come.

D.   Matthew 8:12

But the children of the kingdom shall be cast out into outer darkness: there shall be weeping and gnashing of teeth.

E.   Matthew 28:19

Go ye therefore, and teach all nations, baptizing them in the name of the Father, and of the Son, and of the Holy Ghost.

F.   John 3:3

Jesus answered and said unto him, Verily, verily, I say unto thee, Except a man be born again, he cannot see the kingdom of God.

G.   Romans 10:17

So then faith cometh by hearing, and hearing by the Word of God.

CHAPTER 19

THE LORD'S SUPPER

NEW WORDS

1. Betray — To give someone over to an enemy while pretending to be a friend
2. Actual — Real and true
3. Bodily — With one's body; physically
4. Properly — Correctly; in the right way
5. Confessing Member — A member of church who has made public confession of faith
6. Entire — All; full; whole; with all parts
7. Attend — To go to; to be present at
8. Examine — To look into something very carefully
9. Unworthily — Shamefully; not having the right to; not deserving of
10. Preparatory — In preparation for; getting ready for

THE LORD'S SUPPER

The Lord Jesus gave two sacraments to His New Testament church. The first sacrament is baptism, and the second is the *Lord's supper.*

The very first Lord's supper was served by the Lord Jesus Christ. This took place during His last evening with His apostles. He was *betrayed* later that same night.

And as they were eating, Jesus *took bread,* and blessed it, and brake it, and gave it to the disciples, and said, Take, eat; this is My body.

And He *took the cup,* and gave thanks, and gave it to them, saying, Drink ye all of it;

For this is My blood of the new testament, which is shed for many for the remission of sins.

— Matthew 26:26-28

For I have received of the Lord that which also I delivered unto you, That the Lord Jesus the same night in which He was betrayed took bread:

And when He had given thanks, He brake it, and said, Take, eat: this is My body, which is broken for you: this do in remembrance of Me.

After the same manner also He took the cup, when He had supped, saying, This cup is the new testament in My blood: this do ye, as oft as ye drink it, in remembrance of Me.

For as often as ye *eat this bread, and drink this cup,* ye do shew the Lord's death till He come.

— I Corinthians 11:23-26

Jesus has lovingly commanded His church to continue to use this sacrament until He comes again at the end of the world.

The Lord's supper in the New Testament has taken the place of the passover in the Old Testament. The Old Testament sacraments included blood shedding. They pointed to Christ who would come. The New Testament sacraments do not include blood shedding.

They point back to the blood of Christ which has been shed in full payment for His people's sins.

The signs used in the Lord's supper are:
1. Bread
2. Wine

The **bread,** which is broken, points to Christ's broken body. The **wine,** which is poured, speaks of the blood of Christ which was poured out in His death. The bread and wine are signs of the death of Christ's body.

We need food and drink to stay alive and strong. Our bodies cannot live very long without food and drink.

> And as they did eat, Jesus took **bread,** and blessed it, and brake it, and gave to them, and said, Take, eat: this is My body.
> And He took the **cup,** and when He had given thanks, He gave it to them: and they all drank of it.
> And He said unto them, This is My blood of the New Testament, which is shed for many.
>
> — Mark 14:22-24

Those who are born again are spiritually alive. They love God from their hearts. Their deepest wants and desires are to turn away from sin and love God above all.

Their spiritual life and strength come from Jesus Christ. Jesus **died** for them as their Substitute. Now they may **live** spiritually because of His death. Do you remember what a substitute is? How is Jesus the Substitute of His children? You may wish to read the story on page 24 again.

The bread and wine in the Lord's supper point to Christ's death. God's people find their life and strength in Jesus Christ and His death for them.

> For I determined not to know any thing among you, **save Jesus Christ,** and Him crucified.
> — I Corinthians 2:2

Jesus is the "bread" and "wine," the "food" and "drink," of their spiritual life. Jesus Christ is their spiritual strength.

> Then Jesus said unto them, Verily, verily, I say unto you, Moses gave you not that bread from heaven; but My Father giveth you **the true bread** from heaven.
> For the **bread of God** is He which cometh down from heaven, and giveth life unto the world.
> Then said they unto Him, Lord, evermore give us this bread.
> And Jesus said unto them, **I am the bread of life:** he that cometh to Me shall never hunger; and he that believeth on Me shall never thirst.
>
> **I am the bread of life.**
> Your fathers did eat manna in the wilderness, and are dead.
> This is the **bread which cometh down from heaven,** that a man may eat thereof, and not die.
> I am the **living bread** which came down from heaven: if any man eat of this bread, he shall live for ever: and the bread that I will give is My flesh, which I will give for the life of the world.
> — John 6:32-35; 48-51

WHAT DO YOU THINK?

THE NEED FOR FOOD

Mrs. Renders was seriously sick in the hospital. Everyday her children and grandchildren came to see her. They always asked the doctor if there were any signs of improvement.

One day when they arrived at the hospital, they heard that she had eaten something. The entire family was very glad to hear this news. Why would they be so glad to hear this?

On Whom do we need to "feed" for spiritual life? If a person is "eating" and "drinking" Christ spiritually, why is this such a good sign and such good news?

The Lord's supper is not only a sign but also a seal. It proves the truth of something. The Lord's supper seals these two truths to God's children:

1. That as surely as they see the bread being broken and the wine being poured, so surely is it true that *Christ broke His body and poured out His blood for them.*

2. That as surely as they eat the bread and drink the wine, so surely is it true that *Christ will feed and strengthen them spiritually.*

WHAT DO YOU THINK?

A SIGN AND SEAL

The following questions and answers are from the Heidelberg Catechism. Can you find where the instructor speaks about the *sign* and the *seal* in the Lord's supper?

Q. 75. How art thou admonished and assured in the Lord's Supper, that thou art a partaker of that one sacrifice of Christ, accomplished on the cross, and of all His benefits?

A. Thus: That Christ has commanded me and all believers, to eat of this broken bread, and to drink of this cup, in remembrance of Him, adding these promises: first, that His body was offered and broken on the cross for me, and His blood shed for me, as certainly as I see with my eyes, the bread of the Lord broken for me, and the cup communicated to me; and further, that He feeds and nourishes my soul to everlasting life, with His crucified body and shed blood, as assuredly as I receive from the hands of the minister, and taste with my mouth the bread and cup of the Lord, as certain signs of the body and blood of Christ.

The bread used in the Lord's supper is plain bread. The wine used is normal wine. During the sacrament, the bread remains bread and the wine remains wine. The bread and wine do not change into anything else.

There are churches which teach that the bread and wine in the Lord's supper actually change into the body and blood of Jesus. They teach that a priest actually sacrifices Jesus upon an altar in the church. When people eat this bread, they believe that they eat the *actual* body of Christ.

This is not true. Had Jesus died yet when He said, "This is My body," and "This is My blood"? Why could He not have meant His actual body and blood? What did He mean? Read the "What Do You Think?" on the next page to help answer this last question.

WHAT DO YOU THINK?

HER FIRST "MASS"

Lisa is a twelve-year-old girl. She attends a church which believes in the "Mass." This "Mass" replaces the Lord's supper as a sacrament in her church. When the "Mass" is served, she believes that the bread actually changes into the body of Christ. She believes that she is worshipping Christ as she actually eats His body. Lisa will attend her first "Mass" now that she is twelve years old.

The bread used in this church is baked into hard circles called "wafers". Why would breaking normal bread be dangerous if it actually became the body of Christ? If some crumbs fell to the ground what would this mean? Only the priest drinks the wine in this church. What would happen if the cup was passed and some wine spilled?

Why is it so sad to know that Lisa actually believes these things?

WHAT DO YOU THINK?

I AM THE TRUE VINE

Jesus said,

I am the true vine, and My Father is the husbandman.

Every branch in Me that beareth not fruit He taketh away: and every branch that beareth fruit, He purgeth it, that it may bring forth more fruit. — John 15:1-2

Did Jesus mean that He is an actual vine? Is His Father an actual husbandman of actual vines? Are His people actual branches which bring forth fruit? What did Jesus mean?

I AM THE DOOR

Jesus said,

Verily, verily, I say unto you, I am the door of the sheep.

I am the door: by Me if any man enter in, he shall be saved, and shall go in and out, and find pasture.   — John 10:7b-9

Did Jesus mean that He is an actual door for actual sheep? Can people actually find pasture land in Him? What did Jesus mean?

THIS IS MY BODY

And as they were eating, Jesus took bread, and blessed it, and brake it, and gave it to the disciples, and said, Take, eat; this is My body.

And He took the cup, and gave thanks, and gave it to them, saying, Drink ye all of it;

For this is My blood of the new testament, which is shed for many for the remission of sins.   — Matthew 26:26-28

Did Jesus mean that His disciples were eating His actual body and drinking His actual blood? Had Christ died yet? What did Jesus mean?

Jesus' body is in heaven. It is not on earth anymore. Jesus will come again **bodily** on the final judgment day, but not until that time. Jesus' body, therefore, cannot actually be in a church.

In My Father's house are many mansions: if it were not so, I would have told you. *I go to prepare a place for you.*

And if I go and prepare a place for you, I will come again, and receive you unto Myself; that where I am, there ye may be also.

— John 14:2-3

And it came to pass, while He blessed them, He was parted from them, and *carried up into heaven.*

— Luke 24:51

And when He had spoken these things, while they beheld, *He was taken up;* and a cloud received Him out of their sight.

And while they looked stedfastly toward heaven as He went up, behold, two men stood by them in white apparel;

Which also said, Ye men of Galilee, why stand ye gazing up into heaven? this same *Jesus, which is taken up from you into heaven,* shall so come in like manner as ye have seen Him go into heaven.

— Acts 1:9-11

Who is *gone into heaven,* and is on the right hand of God; angels and authorities and powers being made subject unto Him.

— I Peter 3:22

Jesus' death and sacrifice are complete. His one death paid the full price for the sins of all those who will be saved. Jesus does not need to be sacrificed again and again.

Nor yet that He should offer Himself often, as the high priest entereth into the holy place every year with blood of others.

For then must He often have suffered since the foundation of the world: but now *once* in the end of the world hath *He appeared to put away sin by the sacrifice of Himself.*
— Hebrews 9:25-26

Who being the brightness of His glory, and the express image of His person, and, upholding all things by the word of His power, when *He had by Himself purged our sins,* sat down on the right hand of the Majesty on high.
— Hebrews 1:3

Now where remission of these is, there is *no more offering for sin.*   — Hebrews 10:18

The bread and wine in the Lord's supper are signs which **point to** the body and blood of Christ; but they are **not actually** His body and blood.

To *properly* eat and drink the Lord's supper, a person must have a:

1. Church Right

2. Divine Right

To have a *church right* means that:

WHAT DO YOU THINK?

JESUS' PRESENCE AT THE LORD'S SUPPER

Is Jesus present at the Lord's supper? If His body is in heaven, how then can He be present?

How can question and answer 47 of the Heidelberg Catechism help you answer this question?

Is not Christ then with us even to the end of the world, as He hath promised?

Christ is very man and very God; with respect to His human nature, He is no more on earth; but with respect to His Godhead, majesty, grace, and spirit, He is at no time absent from us.

1. The person is a *confessing member* of the church. He has made public confession of faith. He is old enough to properly examine himself to see if he has a divine right. (You can read about this on the following page.)

2. The person may not be living in any public sin or teaching false doctrines. This is a sin which is known by many or the *entire* church. If the consistory is warning him to stop sinning but he does not listen, then he will be told that he may not *attend* the Lord's supper. He is openly showing the church that he wishes to live in the way of sin instead of the way of God.

WHAT DO YOU THINK?

A FULFILLED DESIRE

A twelve-year-old girl was dying from a serious disease. She spoke to her consistory when they visited her. She told them how she longed to be at the Lord's supper in her church before she died! The consistory gave its permission, and this girl, who was very weak by this time, came to the Lord's table.

This made a deep impression upon the entire congregation. Why, do you think?

WHAT DO YOU THINK?

THE LORD'S SUPPER IS FOR GOD'S PEOPLE

I Corinthians 11:23-29:

For I have received of the Lord that which also I delivered unto you, That the Lord Jesus the same night in which He was betrayed took bread:

And when He had given thanks, He brake it, and said, Take, eat: this is My body, which is broken for you: this do in remembrance of Me.

After the same manner also He took the cup, when He had supped, saying, This cup is the new testament in My blood: this do ye, as oft as ye drink it, in remembrance of Me.

For as often as ye eat this bread, and drink this cup, ye do shew the Lord's death till He come.

Wherefore whosoever shall eat this bread, and drink this cup of the Lord, unworthily, shall be guilty of the body and blood of the Lord.

But *let a man examine himself,* and so let him eat of that bread, and drink of that cup.

For he that eateth and drinketh unworthily, eateth and drinketh damnation to himself, not discerning the Lord's body.

For whom is Christ's body broken? For whom is His blood shed? Who know Him and can "remember" Him as their Savior?

Why must we examine ourselves? Who are invited to the Lord's table?

To properly eat and drink at the Lord's supper, we need not only a church right, but also a divine right.

Having a **divine right** means that we are spiritual children of God. We need to have our hearts renewed and converted from living for ourselves, sin, world, and Satan. We need to be turned and to be living for God. We must love and serve God from our hearts. Our deepest desire must be to do God's will out of love to Him. By nature we selfishly desire to do our own will out of love for ourselves.

If we are converted from a deep love of sin to a deep love of God, we will know something of our:

1. **Misery** — We will feel the weight of our sinfulness. Our sins will bother us. We will painfully learn that our whole heart is sinful and that we cannot make ourselves better, but only sin more.

2. **Deliverance** — We will long and desire to have the Lord Jesus Christ as our Savior. He will become our only hope and trust for salvation because we have learned that we cannot save ourselves.

3. **Thankfulness** — We will desire to love God and walk in a way which pleases Him. We will hate sin and try to flee from it. It will hurt us when we sin against God.

This loving of God and hating of sin will reveal itself in our thoughts, words, and actions.

A person must carefully *examine* himself to see if he has this divine right to eat and drink at the Lord's table. If he has a divine right, he should go to the Lord's table. If he does not have a divine right, he may not eat and drink at the Lord's table.

This self-examination is very important. What do the following verses say about self-examination?

> Wherefore whosoever shall eat this bread, and drink this cup of the Lord, unworthily, shall be guilty of the body and blood of the Lord.
> But let a man examine himself, and so let him eat of that bread, and drink of that cup.
> For he that eateth and drinketh unworthily, eateth and drinketh damnation to himself, not discerning the Lord's body.
>
> — I Corinthians 11:27-29

Do you see how clearly and powerfully God commands us to examine ourselves? Do you see how He warns us not to eat and drink at His table *unworthily?*

To properly eat and drink at the Lord's table, a person needs both a church right and a divine right. Two elders stand at the table when the Lord's supper is served. These elders are called "table waiters" or "table watchers." They must make sure that those without a *church right* do not come to the Lord's table. The table waiters cannot judge if a person has a *divine right* for they cannot see the person's heart. The divine right is a matter between God and the soul of each person. Only God can judge the divine right.

WHAT DO YOU THINK?

SELF-EXAMINATION

The form for administering the Lord's supper speaks of true self-examination as follows:

The true examination of ourselves consists of these three parts:

First. That every one consider by himself, his sins and the curse due to him for them, to the end that he may abhor and humble himself before God: considering that the wrath of God against sin is so great, that (rather than it should go unpunished) He hath punished the same in His beloved Son Jesus Christ, with the bitter and shameful death of the cross.

Secondly. That every one examine his own heart, whether he doth believe this faithful promise of God, that all his sins are forgiven him only for the sake of the passion and death of Jesus Christ, and that the perfect righteousness of Christ is imputed and freely given him as his own, yea, so perfectly, as if he had satisfied in his own person for all his sins, and fulfilled all righteousness.

Thirdly. That every one examine his own conscience, whether he purposeth henceforth to show true thankfulness to God in his whole life, and to walk uprightly before Him; as also, whether he hath laid aside unfeignedly all enmity, hatred, and envy, and doth firmly resolve henceforward to walk in true love and peace with his neighbor.

All those, then, who are thus disposed, God will certainly receive in mercy, and count them worthy partakers of the table of His Son Jesus Christ. On the contrary, those who do not feel this testimony in their hearts, eat and drink judgment to themselves.

Can you find where it speaks of misery, deliverance, and thankfulness in this explanation?

125

No person is "good enough" or "worthy" of himself to eat and drink at the Lord's table. Those who partake of the Lord's supper are not "better" people than those who do not.

Those who properly go to the Lord's table are sinners in themselves; but by God's grace, they seek their righteousness and worthiness outside themselves in Jesus Christ. They are nothing but sinners, but they desire Jesus Christ and long for salvation through Him. They do not honor themselves at the Lord's supper, but they honor their Savior, Jesus Christ. They desire to remember that Christ, by His death, has paid the full price for their sins.

Every adult member in church makes a confession when the Lord's supper is served. By eating and drinking at the Lord's table, a person confesses that he knows something of his sinful misery, deliverance in Christ, and thankfulness to God in his life. He confesses that God has renewed and turned him from loving sin to loving Him.

By not going to the Lord's table, a person confesses that he does not yet believe that God has truly converted him. He confesses that he is yet a stranger of experiencing true misery, deliverance, and thankfulness in his life. Can you see how each person makes a confession when the Lord's supper is served? Can you see how both confessions are very serious confessions?

WHAT DO YOU THINK?

LOVE TO OUR NEIGHBOR

Some Nigerian missionaries planned to have a combined Lord's supper service for several villages in their area. A friend of one of the missionaries, who had been in that area fifteen years before, was also there. This friend asked permission to speak to the people before the service started.

He said, "It is so wonderful to be here today and to see you coming together for this service. Fifteen years ago I was also here. Then you had not yet received the Word of God. At that time you would not have dared to walk into another village because you were constantly at war with each other. And now . . . I see you coming together, sitting together, and soon some of you will be eating at the Lord's table together! God is almighty and His Word is most powerful!"

If a sinner is converted and truly loves God, how will this love overflow to his neighbor? If we are at peace with God through Christ's work, why will this cause us to be at peace with others? Those who sit at the Lord's table must also love one another. Why? — Adapted from *3,000 Illustrations for Christian Service*

A **preparatory** sermon is preached a week before the Lord's supper is served. This sermon is to help each person properly examine himself. The marks of conversion taught in the Bible are misery, deliverance, and thankfulness. These marks must be clearly explained in this sermon. Each person must carefully examine himself according to these marks.

If you were a confessing member with a church right, and next Sunday the Lord's supper was to be served, would you be able to properly attend? Would you have a divine right? Do you know something of the marks of true conversion in your life? These are very important questions to examine between the Lord and your own soul. Are you concerned about these things?

MEMORIZATION QUESTIONS

1. What is the visible sign in the Lord's supper?
   Bread and wine.

2. What does the bread signify in the Lord's supper?
   The body of Christ. Matthew 26:26

3. Why is the bread broken?
   Because Christ's body was broken on the cross. I Corinthians 11:24

4. What does the wine signify?
   His blood. Matthew 26:28

— *Borstius' Catechism*
Lesson XXIV, Q. 7-10

CHAPTER CHECK-UP

1. The Lord's supper in the _____ Testament takes the place of the _____ in the Old Testament.

2. The signs used in the Lord's supper are _____ and wine. They point to Christ's _____ which was broken and his _____ which was poured out to pay the full price for the _____ of His people.

3. How is Jesus the spiritual "food" and "drink" of His people? What does this mean? _____

    _____

4. What two things are sealed to true believers in the Lord's supper?

    a. _____

    _____

    b. _____

    _____

5. How do we know that the bread and wine in the Lord's supper do not actually change into the body and blood of Christ?

    _____

    _____

    _____

6. To properly eat and drink at the Lord's table, we must have a _____ right and a _____ right.

CHAPTER CHECK-UP

7. A church right means:

   a. _____

   _____

   b. _____

   _____

8. A divine right means: _____

   _____

   _____

9. Name three things of which we must know and experience something in our lives, if we are truly converted to God:

   a. _____

   b. _____

   c. _____

10. Who are the "table waiters" and what is their duty during the Lord's supper?

    _____

    _____

11. Why is a "preparatory sermon" preached before the Lord's supper is served?

    _____

    _____

12. What confession is made at the Lord's supper service by:

    a. Confessing members who eat and drink at the Lord's table? _____

    _____

    _____

    b. Confessing members who do not partake of the Lord's supper? _____

    _____

    _____

CHAPTER 20

THE SOUL AFTER DEATH
CHRIST'S SECOND COMING
THE RESURRECTION OF THE DEAD
THE FINAL JUDGMENT
ETERNITY

Man brought death into the world when he sinned against God. Now all people must die, for all have sinned.

However, for God's true children the punishment has been removed from death by their Savior, Jesus Christ. For them,

> For the wages of sin is **death.**
> — Romans 6:23a

> And as it is appointed unto men once **to die,** but after this the judgment.
> — Hebrews 9:27

> Then shall the dust return to the earth as it was: and the **spirit shall return unto God** who gave it.
> — Ecclesiastes 12:7

> And when Jesus had cried with a loud voice, He said, Father, **into Thy hands I commend My spirit:** and having said thus, He gave up the ghost.
> — Luke 23:46

> For dust thou art, and **unto dust shalt thou return.**
> — Genesis 3:19b

death is a way to pass from this sinful world into a sinless heaven. But for those who die in their sins, death is a terrible punishment. Death will bring them into eternal suffering in hell forever.

When a person's body dies, his soul does not. A person's soul leaves his body the moment he dies. The soul returns to God who sends it either to heaven or hell. A person's body returns to dust in the grave.

WHAT DO YOU THINK?

A BELIEVER'S DEATHBED

A young girl who loved God died when she was only nine years old. Before she died, she called her aunt with whom she lived to her bedside. She knew that she would be dying soon.

She said, "Auntie, when I am dead, I would like the minister to preach a sermon to children. He must tell them to ask Jesus for a new heart to love Him. He must tell them to obey their parents, not to tell lies, and to think about having to die. I want the minister to preach about Elisha. He asked the mother of the child that died, 'Is it well?' and his mother answered, 'It is well!' When I die, you may be sad, and others might cry, but you don't have to. It will be well with me, Auntie!"

What is death for those whose sins have been paid for by the death of Jesus Christ? When we see the peaceful way in which this child could die, what lesson can we learn from this story?

— Adapted from *The Shorter Catechism Illustrated*

WHAT DO YOU THINK?

AN UNBELIEVER'S DEATHBED

Voltaire was a famous Frenchman. He spoke and wrote against the Bible and Christianity during his entire life.

A nurse took care of him on his deathbed. She would never again take care of any dying person unless he was a Christian. When asked why, she would answer, "I was the nurse who took care of Voltaire on his deathbed, and for all the money in Europe I would not be willing to see another unbeliever die!"

What is death for those who are still in their sins? What warning is there in this story for us?

— Adapted from *The Shorter Catechism Illustrated*

When God sends souls to heaven or hell, their places are unchangeable. This is why we may not pray for people who have died. Their souls have been sent to their eternal places. This cannot be changed anymore. Can you see this truth in the story about the rich man and Lazarus on the following page?

Why is the time of your life on earth so *valuable?* For what should you seek above everything else?

And he said, ***While the child was yet alive, I fasted and wept:*** for I said, Who can tell whether GOD will be gracious to me, that the child may live?

But now he is dead, wherefore should I fast? can I bring him back again? I shall go to him, but he shall not return to me.
— II Samuel 12:22-23

And he said unto Jesus, Lord, remember me when Thou comest into Thy kingdom.

And Jesus said unto him, Verily I say unto thee, ***To day*** shalt thou be with Me in paradise.
— Luke 23:42-43

And these shall go away ***into everlasting punishment:*** but the righteous ***into life eternal.***
— Matthew 25:46

CHRIST'S SECOND COMING

The Lord Jesus will return from heaven to earth again. He will return in His human nature. The Bible tells us four things about His **second coming.**

1.   Christ will come again **bodily.**

> Which also said, Ye men of Galilee, why stand ye gazing up into heaven? **this same Jesus,** which is taken up from you into heaven, **shall so come in like manner** as ye have seen Him go into heaven.
> — Acts 1:11

> When **Christ,** who is our life, **shall appear,** then shall ye also appear with Him in glory.
> — Colossians 3:4

2.   **Everyone will see** Christ when He returns.

> Behold, He cometh with clouds: and **every eye shall see Him,** and they also which pierced Him: and all kindreds of the earth shall wail because of Him. Even so, Amen.
> — Revelation 1:7

> And **ye shall see** the Son of man sitting on the right hand of power, and coming in the clouds of heaven.
> — Mark 14:62b

3.   Christ's second coming will be with **great power and glory.**

> And then shall appear the sign of the Son of man in heaven: and then shall all the tribes of the earth mourn, and they shall see the Son of man coming in the clouds of heaven with **power and great glory.**
> — Matthew 24:30

> And then shall they see the Son of man coming in a cloud with **power and great glory.**
> — Luke 21:27

WHAT DO YOU THINK?

THE FINAL DESTINATION

We can read about a certain rich man and a certain beggar named Lazarus in:

Luke 16:19-26:
There was a certain rich man, which was clothed in purple and fine linen, and fared sumptuously every day:
And there was a certain beggar named Lazarus, which was laid at his gate full of sores,
And desiring to be fed with the crumbs which fell from the rich man's table: moreover the dogs came and licked his sores.
And it came to pass, that the beggar died, and was carried by the angels into Abraham's bosom: the rich man also died, and was buried;
And in hell he lift up his eyes, being in torments, and seeth Abraham afar off, and Lazarus in his bosom.
And he cried and said, Father Abraham, have mercy on me, and send Lazarus, that he may dip the tip of his finger in water, and cool my tongue; for I am tormented in this flame.
But Abraham said, Son, remember that thou in thy lifetime receivedst thy good things, and likewise Lazarus evil things: but now he is comforted, and thou art tormented.
And beside all this, between us and you there is a great gulf fixed: so that they which would pass from hence to you cannot; neither can they pass to us, that would come from thence.

How can we see from this story that each soul is sent immediately to heaven or hell after the person's body dies? How can we see from this story that each soul's place is unchangeable?

133

EVERY EYE!

Mr. Williams was the mayor of a small town. He hardly ever went to church. Instead, he spent his time playing cards, singing, and dancing. He only wanted to have a "good time."

One Sunday evening, however, he went to hear a new minister. The text was from Revelation 1:7, "Behold, He cometh with clouds, and every eye shall see Him." Mr. Williams was struck with the truth of God's Word as suddenly and powerfully as a person hit with an arrow.

He could no longer live as he had before. When his former friends asked about it, he said, "If you will listen patiently, I will tell you why I go to church. I will tell you why I do not play cards with you anymore. I went to hear the new minister. His text was 'Behold, He cometh with clouds, and every eye shall see Him.' Your eye, too, shall see Him." As he spoke, he pointed to each of them, saying, "Your eye," and "Your eye." They clearly understood his reasons, and never asked him about it again.

How should our knowing that "every eye shall see Him" affect our lives? Why will some long to see Him and others be filled with terror at the sight of Him?

— Adapted from *The NRC Banner of Truth*

4. Christ will come again *suddenly.*

And then shall He send His angels, and shall gather together His elect from the four winds, from the uttermost part of the earth to the uttermost part of heaven.
But *of that day and that hour knoweth no man,* no, not the angels which are in heaven, neither the Son, but the Father.
— Mark 13:27, 32

For as in the days that were before the flood they were eating and drinking, marrying and giving in marriage, until the day that Noe entered into the ark,
And *knew not until the flood came, and took them all away:* so shall also the coming of the Son of man be.
— Matthew 24:38-39

No one knows exactly when Christ will return. Therefore, each person should be prepared. Furthermore, God judges each soul when a person's body dies. This can happen at any time for no one knows when he will die. When we die, our souls will return to God to be judged by Him. Therefore, the day of our death will be a great "judgment day" for us. We must all be prepared for that great day.

Blessed are those servants, whom the lord when he cometh *shall find watching:* verily I say unto you, that he shall gird himself, and make them to sit down to meat, and will come forth and serve them.
And if he shall come in the second watch, or come in the third watch, and find them so, blessed are those servants.
And this know, that if the goodman of the house had known what hour the thief would come, he would have watched, and not have suffered his house to be broken through.
Be ye therefore ready also: for the Son of man cometh at an hour when ye think not.
— Luke 12:37-40

The greatest difference between people will be seen when Christ returns. God's true children will love His appearing. It will be a glorious and wonderful day for them. It will be a day when they will see and be with God whom they love above all.

However, for those who are unconverted, for those who have loved self, sin, and world above all else during their entire lives, this day will be a terrible day. Their fear and terror of meeting a holy and righteous God will have no *limits.*

> And then shall they see the Son of man coming in a cloud with power and great glory.
> And when these things begin to come to pass, then *look up, and lift up your heads: for your redemption draweth nigh.*
> — Luke 21:27-28

> And the kings of the earth, and the great men, and the rich men, and the chief captains, and the mighty men, and every bondman, and every free man, hid themselves in the dens and in the rocks of the mountains;
> And said to the mountains and rocks, Fall on us, and *hide us from the face of Him that sitteth on the throne, and from the wrath of the Lamb:*
> For the great day of His wrath is come: and *who shall be able to stand?*
> — Revelation 6:15-17

Will Christ's return to earth be a day of great happiness or of great fear for you?

THE RESURRECTION OF THE DEAD

When the Lord Jesus will return upon the clouds of heaven, all the graves will be opened. All those who have ever died shall rise again. This great happening is called "the *resurrection.*"

Everyone's body shall be raised, the righteous as well as the wicked. Everyone shall stand before Christ to be judged in soul and body.

WHAT DO YOU THINK?

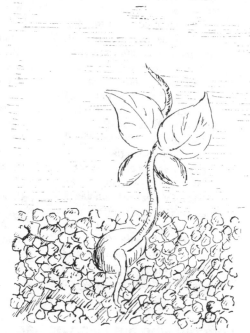

HOW ARE THE DEAD RAISED UP?

The Apostle Paul answered the question, "How are the dead raised up?". He used the example of a seed being planted in the earth and a living plant growing from it later.

> But some man will say, How are the dead raised up? and with what body do they come?
> Thou fool, that which thou sowest is not quickened, except it die:
> And that which thou sowest, thou sowest not that body that shall be, but bare grain, it may chance of wheat, or of some other grain:
> But God giveth it a body as it hath pleased him, and to every seed his own body.
>
> So also is the resurrection of the dead. It is sown in corruption; it is raised in incorruption:
> It is sown in dishonour; it is raised in glory: it is sown in weakness; it is raised in power:
> It is sown a natural body; it is raised a spiritual body. There is a natural body, and there is a spiritual body.
> — I Corinthians 15:35-38; 42-44

How is this a beautiful example of the resurrection? How can we see the miracle of resurrection in a living plant growing from a buried seed?

Marvel not at this: for the hour is coming, in the which all that are in the graves shall hear His voice,

And shall come forth; they that have done good, unto the *resurrection of life*; and they that have done evil, unto the *resurrection of damnation*.

— John 5:28-29

Jesus saith unto her, Thy brother shall rise again.

Martha saith unto Him, I know that he shall rise again in the *resurrection at the last day*.

— John 11:23-24

For if we believe that Jesus died and rose again, even so *them also which sleep in Jesus will God bring with Him*.

— I Thessalonians 4:14

But this I confess unto thee, that after the way which they call heresy, so worship I the God of my fathers, believing all things which are written in the law and in the prophets:

And have hope toward God, which they themselves also allow, that there shall be a *resurrection of the dead*, both of the just and unjust.

— Acts 24:14-15

Now if Christ be preached that He rose from the dead, how say some among you that there is no *resurrection of the dead*?

But if there be no resurrection of the dead, then is Christ not risen:

And if Christ be not risen, then is our preaching vain, and your faith is also vain.

— I Corinthians 15:12-14

And this is the Father's will which hath sent Me that of all which He hath given Me, I should lose nothing, but should *raise it up again at the last day*.

— John 6:39

And I saw the dead, small and great, stand before God and the books were opened and another book was opened, which is the book of life: and the dead were judged out of those things which were written in the books, according to their works.

And *the sea gave up the dead* which were in it; and *death and hell delivered up the dead* which were in them: and they were judged every man according to their works.

— Revelations 20:12-13

All people who are living on earth at the time of Christ's second coming will not die. They will be changed into their eternal bodies in a moment of time.

Behold, I shew you a mystery; We shall not all sleep, but *we shall all be changed,*

In a moment, *in the twinkling of an eye,* at the last trump: for the trumpet shall sound, and the dead shall be raised incorruptible, and we shall be changed.

For this corruptible must put on incorruption, and this mortal must put on immortality.

So when this corruptible shall have put on incorruption, and *this mortal shall have put on immortality,* then shall be brought to pass the saying that is written, Death is swallowed up in victory.

— I Corinthians 15:51-54

For the Lord Himself shall descend from heaven with a shout, with the voice of an archangel, and with the trump of God: and *the dead in Christ shall rise first:*

Then we which are alive and remain shall be caught up together with them in the clouds, to meet the Lord in the air: and so shall we ever be with the Lord.

— I Thessalonians 4:16-17

After the resurrection a person's body will be:

1. **The same.** His body will be the same body he had before he died. It will not be a new body, but his own body brought back to life.

For I know that my Redeemer liveth, and that He shall stand at the latter day upon the earth:

And though after my skin worms destroy *this body, yet in my flesh* shall I see God:

Whom I shall see for myself, and mine eyes shall behold, and not another; though my reins be consumed within me.

— Job 19:25-27

Thy dead men shall live, *together with my dead body shall they arise.*

— Isaiah 26:19a

And as they thus spake, Jesus Himself stood in the midst of them, and saith unto them, Peace be unto you.

Behold My hands and My feet, that it is I Myself: handle Me, and see; *for a spirit hath not flesh and bones,* as ye see Me have.

And when He had thus spoken, He shewed them His hands and His feet.

— Luke 24:36, 39-40

2. **Different.** A person's body after the resurrection will be never-aging and never-dying. It will be a body made to fit his eternal home.

God's children will arise with glorious bodies. They will never again experience tiredness, sickness, or pain. They will have wonderful bodies, fitted for their wonderful life in heaven. The Bible does not tell us exactly what the resurrected bodies of the children of God will be like, but it does tell us the following:

So also is the resurrection of the dead. It is sown in corruption; it is **raised in incorruption:**

It is sown in dishonour; it is **raised in glory:** it is sown in weakness; it is **raised in power:**

It is sown a natural body; it is **raised a spiritual body.** There is a natural body, and a spiritual body.

And so it is written, The first man Adam was made a living soul; the last Adam was made a quickening Spirit.

Howbeit that was not first which is spiritual, but that which is natural; and afterward that which is spiritual.

The first man is of the earth, earthy: the second man is the Lord from heaven.

As is the earthy, such are they also that are earthy; and as is the heavenly, such are they also that are heavenly.

And as we have borne the image of the earthy, we shall also **bear the image of the heavenly.**

Now this I say, brethren, that flesh and blood cannot inherit the kingdom of God; neither doth corruption inherit incorruption.

Behold, I shew you a mystery; We shall not all sleep, but we shall all be changed,

In a moment, in the twinkling of an eye, at the last trump: for the trumpet shall sound, and **the dead shall be raised incorruptible,** and we shall be changed.

For this corruptible must put on **incorruption,** and this mortal must put on **immortality.**

— I Corinthians 15:42-53

For our conversation is in heaven; from whence also we look for the Saviour, the Lord Jesus Christ:

Who shall change our vile body, that it may be fashioned **like unto His glorious body,** according to the working whereby He is able even to subdue all things unto Himself.

— Philippians 3:20-21

THE FINAL JUDGMENT

Immediately after the resurrection, the **final judgment** of all people will take place. Jesus Christ will be the great Judge. He will judge both the righteous and the wicked. All those who have learned to know their own sinfulness and have fled to Jesus Christ will be pronounced innocent by Him. They will

WHAT DO YOU THINK?

SAFETY FROM FIRE

Early settlers on the prairies lived in fear of prairie fires. During the dry summer season, there was great danger of fire starting in the long, dry grass. If a fire started, the strong prairie winds quickly whipped it into a tremendous fury.

Many miles of grass were burned in this way. People lost their homes and even their lives. Nothing could stop or turn such a large wind-whipped fire.

Some people were able to save their lives, however. When they saw the large fire coming, they quickly set fire to their own fields. By the time the prairie fire reached them, they could safely gather in the center of their own fields which were already burned. The great prairie fire would pass around them, but not touch them.

Is the great fire of God's wrath against sin approaching? Where and upon whom has the fire of God's wrath against sin already burned? Why can we find safety there? Why is it the only place of refuge in the great judgment day?

— Adapted from *2,400 Scripture Outlines, Anecdotes, Notes, and Quotes*

I WILL BE LOST FOREVER!

Charles IX was the king of France. He ordered the death of many God-fearing Christians called "Huguenots." In one awful day, 15,000 Huguenots were killed in Paris.

On his deathbed, in the last hours of his life, Charles IX cried out to his doctors, "Asleep or awake, I see the mangled forms of the Huguenots passing before me! They drip with blood and they point at their open wounds. Oh, if only I had at least spared the children! But now, all that blood! I know not where I am. How will it end with me? What shall I do? I will be lost forever! Oh, I have done wrong, I know it!"

How is this a terrible example of how a person's life will pass before him on the judgment day? On that day, we will only be able to stand before God if Jesus Christ is our great Substitute. Why?

— Adapted from *3,000 Illustrations for Christian Service*

be innocent because Christ has paid all their debts. He has earned perfect righteousness for them.

> For *we must all appear before the judgement seat of Christ;* that every one may receive the things done in his body, according to that he hath done, whether it be good or bad.
> — II Corinthians 5:10

> For the Son of man shall come in the glory of His Father with His angels: and then he *shall reward every man* according to his works.
> — Matthew 16:27

> But why dost thou judge thy brother? or why dost thou set at nought thy brother? for *we shall all stand before the judgement seat of Christ.*
> — Romans 14:10

Those who are outside of Jesus Christ, the only Savior of lost sinners, will need to give an *account* of all their thoughts, words, and deeds. God will open their consciences. Their entire lives will pass before them in a moment. They will see everything which happened in their lives.

Who can imagine what it will be to stand before a perfectly holy and righteous God, without Christ as our Substitute, to answer for all our sins!

> But I say unto you, That every idle word that men shall speak, they shall give account thereof *in the day of judgment.*
> — Matthew 12:36

> For we know Him that hath said, Vengeance belongeth unto Me, I will recompense, saith the Lord. And again, *The Lord shall judge His people.*
> It is a fearful thing to fall into the hands of the living God.
> — Hebrews 10:30-31

> And the kings of the earth, and the great men, and the rich men, and the chief captains, and the mighty men, and every bondman, and every free man, hid themselves in the dens and in the rocks of the mountains;
> And said to the mountains and rocks, Fall on us, and hide us from the face of Him that sitteth on the throne, and from the wrath of the Lamb:
> For *the great day of His wrath* is come: and who shall be able to stand?
> — Revelation 6:15-17

> For God shall bring every work *into judgment,* with every secret thing, whether it be good, or whether it be evil.
> — Ecclesiastes 12:14

As Judge, Christ will **pronounce** His just sentence upon all people. He will say to those on His right hand:

> **Come,** ye blessed of My Father, **inherit the kingdom** prepared for you from the foundation of the world.
> — Matthew 25:34b

Then He will turn and condemn those on His left by saying:

> **Depart,** from Me, ye cursed, **into everlasting fire,** prepared for the devil and his angels.
> — Matthew 25:41b

What a great difference between people will be seen on the judgment day! Where will you stand? Will you be on the right hand or on the left? Are you seeking for or have you found salvation in Jesus Christ?

WHAT DO YOU THINK?

WHO SEES IT?

One night long ago, a man went out with his little boy to steal some corn. They crept quietly into a cornfield along the road. They looked in all directions to see if anyone was watching them.

The father was about to fill his bag with corn when the little boy suddenly whispered to him, "Daddy, you forgot to look up."

This remark sank into the father's heart. It reminded him that there was an all-seeing, all-knowing God above. Together they left the cornfield with an empty bag.

Why was this boy's remark true? When would this deed have come back in the minds of this father and son?

— Adapted from **The NRC Banner of Truth**

WHAT DO YOU THINK?

NO PROFIT FROM SIN

Rev. William Jay was taking a walk in the country on a warm day. He stopped to watch a thresher hard at work. Seeing the man sweating and working hard, he said to him, "My friend, in all **labor** there is profit."

The man **paused.** Slowly he turned toward the minister and answered, "No sir, that is not completely true." Rev. Jay wondered what the man had in mind. "There is one **exception,**" the man continued. "I have labored in the service of sin for many years, and I have received no profit from it."

The minister and the farmhand had a nice conversation that morning.

How is this man's answer true? What are the wages of sin? What does God say about this in Romans 6:23?

— Adapted from **The Shorter Catechism Illustrated**

WHAT DO YOU THINK?

NO WEDDING GARMENT

Read the "Parable of the Marriage Feast of the King's Son" in:

Matthew 22:1-14:

And Jesus answered and spake unto them again by parables, and said,

The kingdom of heaven is like unto a certain king, which made a marriage for his son,

And sent forth his servants to call them that were bidden to the wedding: and they would not come.

Again, he sent forth other servants, saying, Tell them which are bidden, Behold, I have prepared my dinner: my oxen and my fatlings are killed, and all things are ready: come unto the marriage.

But they made light of it, and went their ways, one to his farm, another to his merchandise:

And the remnant took his servants, and entreated them spitefully, and slew them.

But when the king heard thereof, he was wroth: and he sent forth his armies, and destroyed those murderers, and burned up their city.

Then saith he to his servants, The wedding is ready, but they which were bidden were not worthy.

Go ye therefore into the highways, and as many as ye shall find, bid to the marriage.

So those servants went out into the highways, and gathered together all as many as they found, both bad and good, and the wedding was furnished with guests.

And when the king came in to see the guests, he saw there a man which had not on a wedding garment:

And he saith unto him, Friend, how camest thou in hither not having a wedding garment? And he was speechless.

Then said the king to the servants, Bind him hand and foot, and take him away, and cast him into outer darkness; there shall be weeping and gnashing of teeth.

For many are called, but few are chosen.

To what do the following parts of this parable point? Who is the King? Who is His Son? What is the feast? What is the invitation to the feast? Who are the servants who bring this invitation? Who are the people who rejected the invitation? Why did they reject the invitation? What is the wedding garment in this parable (see Revelation 19:8-9 and 7:13-14)? When judged, why was the man without a wedding garment speechless? What is the only right to enter into heaven which a person must have? Where will all others be sent?

ETERNITY

After Christ has righteously judged all people, He will send them, with both body and soul, to their eternal places. Christ will bring His children into heaven. The angels will cast all the ungodly into hell. Hell will be the dwelling place of lost sinners eternally. *Eternity* is much longer than a time of a hundred or a thousand years. It is without end. We know that our final home will be eternal. How does this add to the great importance of it for us?

HELL

Those who are not saved by Jesus Christ will be punished forever in hell for their sins.

Hell is a place where people are:

1. Separated completely from any blessing of God forever.
2. Separated completely from any of God's children forever.
3. With devils and haters of God forever.
4. Tormented by their consciences continually forever.
5. Suffering under the wrath of God poured out against their sins forever.

Hell is a place of great **torment,** pain, and suffering. It is pictured in the Bible as a place of fire. The fire of God's wrath against sin and the fire of their guilty consciences will burn and torment those in hell forever. Those in hell will suffer both in soul and body for they have sinned against God with both.

Then said the king to his servants, Bind him hand and foot, and take him away, and *cast him into outer darkness*; there shall be weeping and gnashing of teeth.

— Matthew 22:13

Where their worm dieth not, and *the fire is not quenched*.

— Mark 9:44

Raging waves of the sea, foaming out their own shame; wandering stars, to whom is reserved the *blackness of darkness for ever*.

— Jude :13

But the fearful, and unbelieving, and the abominable, and murderers, and whoremongers, and sorcerers, and idolators, and all liars, shall have their part in *the lake which burneth with fire and brimstone*: which is the second death.

— Revelation 21:8

So shall it be at the end of the world: The angels shall come forth, and sever the wicked from among the just,

And shall cast them into the *furnace of fire*: there shall be wailing and gnashing of teeth.

— Matthew 13:49-50

The same shall drink of the wine of the wrath of God, which is poured out without mixture into the cup of His indignation; and *he shall be tormented with fire and brimstone* in the presence of the holy angels, and in the presence of the Lamb:

And the smoke of their torment ascendeth up for ever and ever: and *they have no rest day nor night,* who worship the beast and his image, and whosoever receiveth the mark of his name.

— Revelation 14:10-11

A YOUNG CHILD WHO DIED IN THE LORD

A lady who had a God-fearing grandmother married a worldly man. This couple seldom went to church. They never read the Bible. The husband's idol was sports. As time went on, this couple received two daughters. These children never heard about religion except when they visited their great-grandmother.

The second child was very weak. She was often sick, and a serious illness developed.

She was ill for a long time. Her mother became very concerned about her youngest daughter. She gave her all the care she could. She was ready to help her daughter any moment of the day or night.

This excellent care, however, did not help. Jeannie, who was only four years old, was gradually losing her strength. She had no appetite, and hardly slept. She gradually lost weight. At first, the doctor thought she would recover. But after some weeks, he told the parents that she would not live long.

This was a hard blow for the parents. But the mother still tried to encourage her daughter by saying, "Soon you will get healthy again, Jean. Then you can go outside and play with the other girls."

The poor child believed her mother at first. For a while she was more cheerful. This did not last long, however. Jeannie began to realize that her condition was serious. It could very well be that she must die. She became very serious. Jeannie thought more about death than she cared to show.

"What are you thinking about, my dear?"

There was no answer. A few days later, the mother said to her again, "Jeannie, tell me what you are worrying about." Jeannie began to cry.

"Come, my dear, tell me please. . ."

After quite some time, she answered, "Mom, I am a bad girl!"

"A bad girl, how can you say that?" Jeannie still sobbed. "No, you are not a bad girl. You have always been good for Mom and Dad. You were never naughty. How can you say then that you are a bad girl?"

Between her tears and sobbing, she spoke about her inward condition. She pointed to her heart and said, "Mother, I have sinned against God. I know I must die, and dying means meeting God. How can I meet Him when I have so many sins?"

Her mother did not know what to answer. She knew from what she had learned as a child that what her daughter said was true. She had forsaken this truth which Grandmother had taught her.

"Mommy," Jeannie said, "why did you and Daddy never teach me that we must die and meet a holy God? I know I must die, but I cannot die." How she sobbed and cried! The mother sank onto her child's sickbed. Deep feelings of guilt overcame her. She did not know what to answer her dear daughter!

A few minutes later Jeannie said, "Mother, I wish I could speak to a good minister. Do you mind getting one for me?"

The mother knew very well what her young daughter meant by a "good" minister. She knew that there were many preachers who did not speak the truth. She was amazed, however, that her young daughter would be aware of this.

"I know a minister of God in town here," she answered. "I'll call and ask him to visit you."

Jeannie was very happy. A smile came on her face.

The next day a minister visited the sick girl. "Hello, my dear girl. What is your name?" he asked.

"Jeannie."

"You told your mom that you would like to see me.

WHAT DO YOU THINK? (Continued)

What can I do for you?"

"I am afraid you cannot do anything for me, but I have such a burden. I don't know how to explain it."

"What causes your burden, Jeannie?"

"My sins," she answered. "Oh, my sins!" she exclaimed.

Then the minister explained in simple words that forgiveness from sin is possible. The Lord Jesus suffered and died for His people. He shed His blood for them so that all their sins could be washed away.

"Yes," the girl answered, "but did He come for me?"

The minister was pleased with the questions and answers given by the dying girl. He was astonished because he knew she had never been brought up under the truth. He believed that true Godly sorrow for her sins was being worked in her heart by the Holy Spirit.

Before the minister left, he offered a prayer. He asked God to remember the sick girl in mercy. When he shook hands with her, she begged him to come back and pray often for her. The Lord's way, however, was different. The time of her death was near. That same night at about 3 a.m., Jeannie called her mother.

The mother went to see her. "What's wrong, my dear?"

"Oh Mom, I hear singing, such beautiful singing. Do you hear it, Mom?" No, her mother did not hear it. It was the singing of angels which sounded in the child's ear. In the meantime, Father also came to see his little girl. She repeated, "Oh, what beautiful singing!" After a few minutes, she said, "Oh, the Lord is coming to take me! I am going to heaven. Goodbye!" She closed her eyes, and peacefully, Jeannie was gone.

— Adapted from *Religious Stores for Young and Old: Volume IV*

Compare Jeannie's death with the death of the men in the "Lost Men" story on page 141. Why is there such a great difference? Why is this difference the greatest and most important of all possible differences between people?

But ye are come unto Mount Sion, and unto the city of the living God, *the heavenly Jerusalem*, and to an innumerable company of angels,

To the general assembly and church of the firstborn, which are written in heaven, and to God the Judge of all, and to the spirits of just men made perfect,

And to Jesus the Mediator of the new covenant, and to the blood of sprinkling, that speaketh better things than that of Abel.

— Hebrews 12:22-24

Then shall the King say unto them on His right hand, Come, ye blessed of My Father, *inherit the kingdom* prepared for you from the foundation of the world.

— Matthew 25:34

In *My Father's house* are many mansions: if it were not so, I would have told you. I go to prepare a place for you.

— John 14:2

After this I beheld, and, lo, a great multitude, which no man could number, of all nations, and kindreds, and people, and tongues, stood before the throne, and before the Lamb, *clothed with white robes, and palms in their hands*:

And I said unto him, Sir, thou knowest. And he said unto me, These are they which came out of great tribulation, and have washed their robes, and made them white in the blood of the Lamb.

Therefore are they before the throne of God, and *serve Him day and night in His temple*: and He that sitteth on the throne shall dwell among them.

They shall hunger no more, neither thirst any more; neither shall the sun light on them, nor any heat.

For the Lamb which is in the midst of the throne shall feed them, and shall lead them unto living fountains of waters: and *God shall wipe away all tears from their eyes*.

— Revelation 7:9, 14-17

And he shewed me a pure river of water of life, clear as crystal, proceeding out of the throne of God and of the Lamb.

In the midst of the street of it, and on either side of the river, was there a tree of life, which bare twelve manner of fruits, and yielded her fruit every month: and the leaves of the tree were for the healing of the nations.

And there shall be no more curse: but the throne of God and of the Lamb shall be in it: and *His servants shall serve Him*:

And they shall see His face; and His name shall be in their foreheads.

And there shall be no night there; and they need no candle, neither light of the sun; for the Lord God giveth them light: and *they shall reign for ever and ever*.

— Revelation 22:1-5

And I appoint unto you a *kingdom,* as My Father hath appointed unto Me.

— Luke 22:29

It is a *fearful* thing to fall into the hands of the living God.
— Hebrews 10:31

. . . O generation of vipers, who hath warned you to flee from the *wrath to come?*
— Luke 3:7b

The punishment of those in hell will continue forever. Their punishment will be without rest or end. Sinners have sinned against an infinite and eternal God. Their just sentence requires an eternal and infinite payment — a payment which will never end.

And these shall go away into *everlasting punishment:* but the righteous into life eternal.
— Matthew 25:46

Then shall He say also unto them on the left hand, Depart from Me, ye cursed, into *everlasting fire*, prepared for the devil and his angels.
— Matthew 25:41

The same shall drink of the wine of the wrath of God, which is poured out without mixture into the cup of His indignation: and he shall be tormented with fire and brimstone in the presence of the holy angels, and in the presence of the Lamb:

And the smoke of their torment ascendeth up *for ever and ever*: and they have no rest day nor night, who worship the beast and his image, and whosoever receiveth the mark of his name.
— Revelation 14:10-11

It is impossible to describe what hell will be, for it is impossible to say how awful sin is! Sin is open rebellion against God, the eternal Creator of all things.

Therefore, God warns us so clearly to flee from His wrath which will be poured out upon sinners. He calls us to take refuge in His Son, Jesus Christ. It will be terrible to fall into the hands of a holy and justly angry God.

HEAVEN

Those who are saved by Jesus Christ will be brought into heaven. As we cannot fully understand how terrible hell is, so we cannot fully understand how wonderful heaven is.

Heaven is a place of eternal joy. God's children will be full of joy in heaven because there God's people will:

1. **Be perfectly delivered from all their enemies.** Satan, sin, the world, and their old sinful natures will not be in heaven. Christ has delivered them completely and eternally from these enemies. God shall wipe all tears from their eyes. No sin, pain, sorrow, and death will be in heaven.

2. **Perfectly serve and worship God.** In heaven, God's children will serve God without sin. They will perfectly sing and praise God's wonderful name forever.

3. **Walk in the perfect beauty of heaven.** Heaven is a place of great beauty which is not spoiled or damaged by sin. It is a place of many **mansions** prepared by Christ especially for His people. It will always be "day" with no "night" there. The saved shall walk in the most wonderful and beautiful surroundings in heaven.

4. **Be in perfect communion with God.** God's children will enjoy eternal friendship with God in heaven. Sin will not separate them from God's presence anymore. They will continually enjoy knowing, loving, and praising God. They will be with God forever.

THE BROAD AND NARROW WAY

Upon which way are you traveling? How can you know? Where will each path end?

In heaven, God's people will receive the deepest longings and desires of their hearts. There they will love, serve, and praise God perfectly without sin forever.

Where will you stand on the great judgment day? Are your deepest longings and desires still to serve yourself, sin, and this world? Or have you been converted by God so that your deepest longings and desires are to serve and love the Lord? If so, then your thoughts, words, and actions will show this love. You will try to do that which is pleasing to God. There are only two ways. One way leads to heaven, and the other leads to hell. Upon which road are you traveling?

You cannot convert yourself. Therefore seek, pray, and plead with God to save you. Do not rest until you find rest in Jesus Christ as your Savior and King!

MEMORIZATION QUESTIONS

1. Which punishment is this?
   Everlasting destruction.
   II Thessalonians 1:9

2. Where will that be?
   In hell. Luke 16:23

3. What is hell?
   A lake which burneth with fire and brimstone. Revelation 21:8

4. Who will be there?
   Unconverted adults and children.
   Luke 19:27

5. What are the works of the devil?
   Lying, slandering, and murder. John 8:44

6. What does the Lord say about liars?
   That He shall destroy them. Psalm 5:6

7. Can those who do the works of the devil enter heaven?
   No. I Corinthians 6:9,10

8. Who will enter heaven?
   Those who love God and the Lord Jesus Christ. Psalm 65:4

9. What does the Bible assure us of?
   That if we die unconverted we shall come to eternal damnation. John 3:36

10. Do you wish to be there?
    I show by my works that I do.

11. By what kind of conduct do children show this?
    By their disobedience to God and their parents.

12. Where will those children go who remain disobedient?
    With the devils in hell. Luke 16:24

13. What will become of our bodies?
    They will return to the dust and be eaten by the worms. Genesis 3:19c

14. Who only can be called rich?
    Those who have a treasure in heaven. Colossians 1:12

15. Who have a desire to gladly depart from this world?
    Those who have the Lord Jesus as their portion. Philippians 1:23

16. What did Asaph say to them in the seventy-third psalm?
    "Whom have I in heaven, but Thee, and there is none upon earth that I desire beside thee."

17. Who are the most happy people?
    They who know and desire no greater joy than to do God's will. John 4:34

18. Who are the most unhappy people?
    They who continue doing their own will and way.

19. What will be the end of them?
    Eternal destruction.

20. And what will be the end of those who fear God?
    Eternal salvation and glory. Matthew 25:46

Ledeboer's Catechism: Q. 19-22, 54-57, 63-66, 90-97

CHAPTER CHECK-UP

1. What brought death into the world? _____

_____

2. When a person dies, his body goes to _____ and his soul

is sent by God to _____ or to _____.

3. Why is it wrong to pray for someone who has died? _____

_____

4. The Bible tells us that when Christ returns to earth, He will appear in the follow-

ing ways:

a. _____

b. _____

c. _____

d. _____

5. No person knows exactly when Christ will return, therefore each person should

be _____.

6. Why is the day of our death such an important day? _____

_____

_____

7. a. What is the greatest possible difference between people? _____

_____

b. When will this difference be clearly seen? _____

_____

CHAPTER CHECK-UP

8. What will happen when the resurrection takes place? _____

_____

9. Explain how a person's body, after the resurrection, will be:

    a. The same — _____

    _____

    b. Different — _____

    _____

10. Who will judge all people in the final judgment? _____

11. In the final judgment, why will:

    a. God's people be pronounced innocent? _____

    _____

    _____

    b. Unconverted people be pronounced guilty? _____

    _____

12. Hell is a place of great torment and suffering because lost sinners in hell are:

    a. _____

    b. _____

    c. _____

    d. _____

    e. _____

13. Heaven is a place of perfect joy because God's people in heaven are:

    a. _____

    b. _____

    c. _____

    d. _____

14. When we speak of eternity, what is the most important question for each of us? _____

CHAPTER NINETEEN

REVIEW QUESTIONS

1. What are the signs used in the Lord's supper and to what do they point?

   Sign: **Meaning:**

   a. _____   _____

   b. _____   _____

2. a. When the Lord Jesus said, "I am the vine," "I am the door of the sheep," "This is My body," or "This is My blood," did Jesus mean these things actually and physically? _____

   b. What did He mean? _____

   _____

   _____

3. What is meant by a converted person's knowledge of:

   a. Misery? — _____

   _____

   _____

   b. Deliverance? — _____

   _____

   _____

   c. Thankfulness? — _____

   _____

   _____

4. Why is it necessary to know something of our misery, deliverance, and thankfulness to properly participate in the Lord's supper?

   _____

   _____

5. How is a confession made at the Lord's supper service by:

   a. Confessing members who eat and drink at the Lord's table? _____

   _____

   _____

   b. Confessing members who do not participate? _____

   _____

   _____

6. Why is death so different for a converted person than for an unconverted person? _____

_____

_____

7. When a soul is judged and sent to _____ or to _____, its place is _____.

8. a. Who will be filled with great joy at Christ's second coming?

_____ Why? _____

_____

_____

   b. Who will be filled with great fear at Christ's second coming?

_____ Why? _____

_____

_____

9. After the resurrection, the bodies of _____ will be made like _____ glorious body. (See Philippians 3:20-21)

10. On the final judgment day, who are the people that will be placed on Christ's:

    a. Right hand? — _____

    b. Left hand? — _____

11. The fire of _____ and the fire of their guilty _____ will burn and torment those in hell forever.

12. How will God's people receive their deepest longings and desires in heaven?

_____

_____

13. Why are some sinners:

    a. Saved? _____

_____

    b. Lost? _____

_____

FILL IN THE MISSING BLANKS

Fill in the missing letters to complete each of the NEW WORDS in Chapters 19 and 20. Then place the letter of the best matching meaning on the blank provided.

Words

_____ 1. _ _ _ o _ _ _ i _ _

_____ 2. _ e _ _ a _

_____ 3. _ c c _ _ _ _

_____ 4. _ n _ i _ _

_____ 5. _ _ e _ a _ _

_____ 6. _ _ _ e _ _ i _ _

_____ 7. _ o _ i _

_____ 8. _ i _ i _

_____ 9. _ _ r _ e _ _

_____ 10. _ _ a _ i _ _

_____ 11. _ _ u _ e

_____ 12. _ _ _ e _ a _ _ _ _ _

_____ 13. _ _ _ n s _ _ _

_____ 14. _ _ t _ a _

_____ 15. _ a _ o _

_____ 16. _ _ t e _ _

_____ 17. _ _ _ e _ _ e _ _

_____ 18. _ _ o _ e _ _

_____ 19. _ _ o _ o _ _ _ _

_____ 20. _ _ _ _ e _ _ i _ _ _ e
_ _ e _

Meanings

A. Correctly; in the right way

B. In preparation of; getting ready for

C. Real and true

D. An explanation of the details and events

E. Shamefully; not having the right to; not deserving to

F. One who does not believe in Jesus Christ or God's Word

G. Something which does not follow the usual rule or pattern

H. To give something over to an enemy while pretending to be a friend

I. The end or boundary

J. All; whole; with all parts

K. A large and beautiful place in which to live

L. To look into something very carefully

M. To stop for a short time

N. With one's body; physically

O. To speak a sentence of judgment

P. Extreme pain and torture of mind or body

Q. A member of church who has made public confession of faith

R. Having great importance and worth

S. Work

T. To go to; to be present at

BIBLE STUDY QUESTIONS

Draw a line to connect each doctrinal truth with the text which most clearly teaches this truth.

Doctrinal Truths

1. The bread in the Lord's supper points to Christ's body.

2. The wine in the Lord's supper points to Christ's blood.

3. Each person must carefully examine himself to see if he may properly eat and drink at the Lord's table.

4. When a person dies, his soul returns to God and his body returns to dust.

5. Every person will see Christ when He returns to earth with great power and glory.

6. After the resurrection, the bodies of God's children will be more spiritual and glorious than now.

7. Every person will be judged by Christ on the final judgment day.

Texts

A. 1 Corinthians 11:28-29

But let a man examine himself, and so let him eat of that bread, and drink of that cup.

For he that eateth and drinketh unworthily, eateth and drinketh damnation to himself, not discerning the Lord's body.

B. Ecclesiastes 12:7

Then shall the dust return to the earth as it was: and the spirit shall return unto God who gave it.

C. Revelation 1:7

Behold, He cometh with clouds; and every eye shall see Him, and they also which pierced Him: and all kindreds of the earth shall wail because of Him. Even so, Amen.

D. I Corinthians 15:43-44

It is sown in dishonour; it is raised in glory: it is sown in weakness; it is raised in power:

It is sown a natural body; it is raised a spiritual body. There is a natural body, and there is a spiritual body.

E. Matthew 26:26

And as they were eating, Jesus took bread, and blessed it, and brake it, and gave it to the disciples, and said, Take, eat; this is My body.

F. II Corinthians 5:10

For we must all appear before the judgment seat of Christ; that every one may receive the things done in his body, according to that He hath done, whether it be good or bad.

G. Matthew 26:27-28

And He took the cup, and gave thanks, and gave it to them, saying, Drink ye all of it;

For this is My blood of the new testament, which is shed for many for the remission of sins.

MEMORIZATION QUESTION INDEX

PRIMARY SOURCE: *Simple Questions for Children* — Rev. L.G.C. Ledeboer

SECONDARY SOURCES: *Short Questions for Little Children* — Rev. J. Borstius

Bible History in Questions and Answers for Beginners — Rev. P. Dyksterhuis

Rev. Ledeboer's Question *Number*	Bible Doctrine for Younger Children's *Chapter* and *Question* Number	Rev. Ledeboer's Question *Number*	Bible Doctrine for Younger Children's *Chapter* and *Question* Number
1	4-1	47	8-2
2	2-1	48	8-3
3	2-2	49	5-12
4	2-3	50	5-13
5	2-4	51	9-1
6	5-1	52	9-2
7	5-2	53	9-3
8	5-3	53	10-3
9	5-4	54	20-5
10	5-5	55	20-6
11	5-6	56	20-7
12	5-7	57	20-8
13	5-8	58	11-10
14	5-9	59	11-11
15	12-1	60	11-12
16	12-2	60	14-1
17	12-3	61	14-2
18	12-4	62	14-3
19	20-1	63	20-9
20	20-2	64	20-10
21	20-3	65	20-11
22	20-4	66	20-12
23	8-4	67	13-10
24	8-5	68	13-11
25	8-6	69	13-12
26	8-7	70	13-13
27	11-1	71	17-1
28	11-2	72	17-2
29	11-3	73	17-3
30	11-4	73	20-14
31	11-5	74	17-4
32	5-10	74	20-15
33	5-11	75	17-5
34	13-1	76	17-6
35	13-2	77	17-7
36	13-3	78	17-8
37	13-4	79	17-9
38	11-6	80	17-10
39	11-7	80	1-1
40	11-8	81	1-2
41	11-9	82	1-3
42	14-1	83	1-4
43	14-2	84	1-5
44	14-3	85	13-5
45	14-4	86	13-6
46	8-1	87	13-7

MEMORIZATION QUESTION INDEX

Rev. Ledeboer's Question **Number**	Bible Doctrine for Younger Children's **Chapter** and **Question** Number
88	13-8
89	13-9
90	20-13
91	20-14
92	20-15
93	20-16
94	20-17
95	20-18
96	20-19
97	20-20

Rev. Borstius' **Chapter** and Question **Number**	Bible Doctrine for Younger Children's **Chapter** and **Question** Number
17-1	10-1
17-2	10-2
17-3	10-3
19-1	2-5
19-2	2-6
19-3	2-7
22-2	9-4
22-3	9-5
22-4	9-6
22-5	9-7
22-6	9-8
22-8	10-4
22-9	10-5
23-3	12-5
23-4	12-6
23-5	12-7
23-6	12-8
24-1	18-5
24-2	18-6
24-3	18-7
24-4	18-8
24-5	18-9
24-6	18-10
24-7	19-1

Rev. Borstius' **Chapter** and Question **Number**	Bible Doctrine for Younger Children's **Chapter** and **Question** Number
24-8	19-2
24-9	19-3
24-10	19-4
27-1	14-4
27-2	14-5
27-3	14-6
27-4	14-7
27-5	14-8

Rev. Dyksterhuis' **Chapter** and Question **Number**	Bible Doctrine for Younger Children's **Chapter** and **Question** Number
1-1	3-1
1-2	3-2
1-3	3-3
1-4	3-4
1-5	3-5
1-6	3-6
1-7	3-7
1-8	3-8
1-9	3-9
1-10	3-10
2-1	4-2
2-2	4-3
2-3	4-4
2-4	4-5

Scriptural Memorization Passages

Passage	Bible Doctrine for Younger Children's **Chapter**
Exodus 20:1-11	6
Exodus 20:12-17	7
I Corinthians 12:12-14	15
I Corinthians 12:26-28	15
Ephesians 1:3-6	16

DIRECTORY OF SOURCE CREDITS

The Banner of Truth
Rev. W.C. Lamain, Ed.
Banner of Truth
1422 Tamarack Ave. N.W.
Grand Rapids, Michigan
49504

Bible History Presented in Questions and Answers for Beginners
Rev. P. Dyksterhuis
NRC Book and Publishing Committee
55 Robin Hood Way
Wayne, New Jersey
O7470

The Broad and Narrow Way
Marshall, Morgan & Scott
London, England

Cruden's Unabridged Concordance
Alexander Cruden
Baker Book House
P.O. Box No. 6287
Grand Rapids, Michigan
49506

A Hive of Busy Bees
Effie M. Williams
Rod and Staff Publishers, Inc.
Crockett, Kentucky
41413

Missionary Stories and More Missionary Stories
Theresa Worman
Moody Press
2101 West Howard Street
Chicago, Illinois
60645

Religious Stories for Young and Old Vol. II, III, IV
NRC Book and Publishing Committee
55 Robin Hood Way
Wayne, New Jersey
07470

Short Questions for Little Children
Rev. J. Borstius
NRC Book and Publishing Committee
55 Robin Hood Way
Wayne, New Jersey
07470

The Shorter Catechism Illustrated
John Whitecross, Ed.
The Banner of Truth Trust
78b Chilton Street
London, England

Simple Catechism Questions for Children
Rev. L.G.C. Ledeboer
NRC Book and Publishing Committee
55 Robin Hood Way
Wayne, New Jersey
07470

3,000 Illustrations for Christian Service
Walter B. Knight
W.B. Eerdman's Publishing Co.
255 Jefferson Ave. S.E.
Grand Rapids, Michigan
49503

A Treatise of the Compendium
Rev. G.H. Kersten
NRC Book and Publishing Committee
55 Robin Hood Way
Wayne, New Jersey
07470

2,400 Scripture Outlines, Anecdotes, Notes and Quotes
A. Noismith
Baker Book House
P.O. Box No. 6287
Grand Rapids, Michigan
49506

The Wonderful Providence of the Almighty God seen in the Lives of Young and Old
Rev. J. Van Zweden
NRC Book and Publishing Committee
55 Robin Hood Way
Wayne, New Jersey
07470

The Wonders of Creation
Alfred M. Rehwinkel © 1974
Bethany Fellowship Inc.
6820 Auto Club Road
Minneapolis, Minnesota
55438

Youth's Living Ideals
Glen Berry, Ed.
Youth's Living Ideals
Rt. 2
Elon College, N.C.
27244

ASSIGNMENT RECORD

Assignment	Due Date	Completed ✓

NOTES

BIBLE DOCTRINE SCORESHEET

Student's Name: _____

Year: _____

BIBLE DOCTRINE FOR YOUNGER CHILDREN

BOOK E – CHAPTERS 11-20

CHAPTER CHECK-UP AND REVIEW PAGES

	11	12	REVIEW	13	14	REVIEW	15	16	REVIEW	17	18	REVIEW	19	20	REVIEW
A A A–															
B B+ B B–															
C C+ C C–															
D D															
E E															

CHAPTER TESTS

	11	12	13	14	15	16	17	18	19	20
A A A–										
B B+ B B–										
C C+ C C–										
D D										
E E										

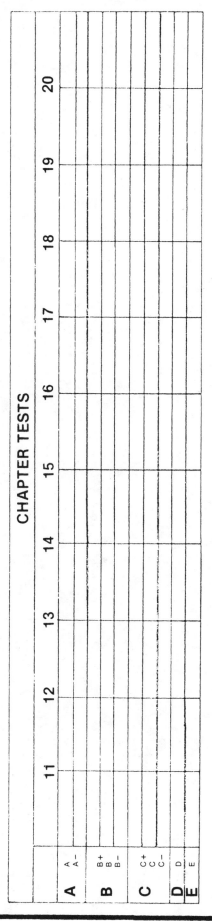

Parent's Signature _____ Unit 12 _____ Unit 16 _____

Unit 14 _____ Unit 18 _____